S0-BIK-233

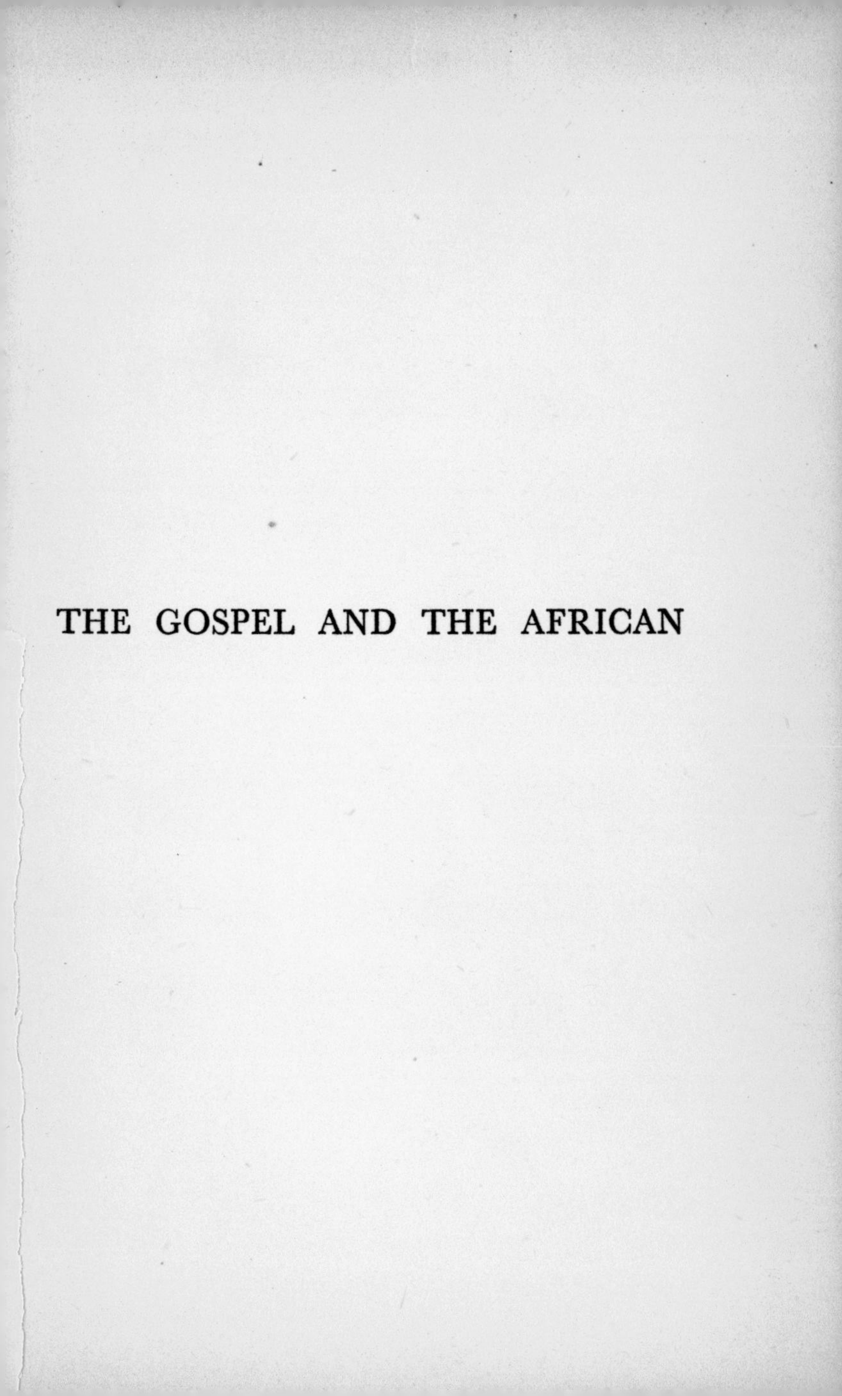

THE GOSPEL AND THE AFRICAN

THE GOSPEL AND THE AFRICAN

The Croall Lectures for 1930–1931

ON

THE IMPACT OF THE GOSPEL ON A CENTRAL AFRICAN PEOPLE

BY THE

REV. ALEXANDER HETHERWICK

C.B.E., D.D.

LATE HEAD OF THE BLANTYRE MISSION, NYASALAND, CENTRAL AFRICA

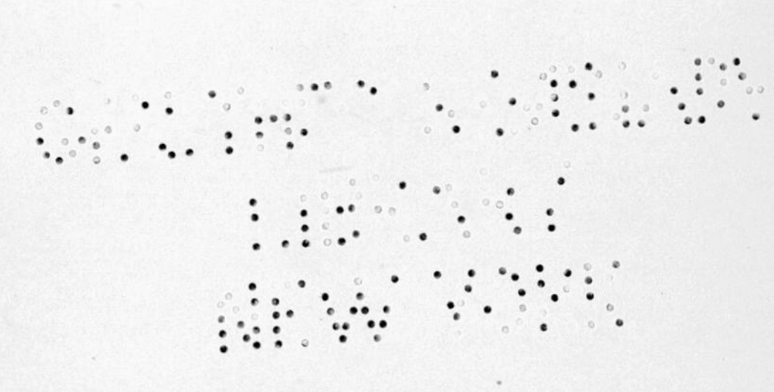

EDINBURGH: T. & T. CLARK, 38 GEORGE STREET

1932

PRINTED IN GREAT BRITAIN BY
MORRISON AND GIBB LIMITED
FOR
T. & T. CLARK, EDINBURGH
LONDON: SIMPKIN MARSHALL, LIMITED
NEW YORK: CHARLES SCRIBNER'S SONS

TO

HIS FELLOW-WORKERS ON THE STAFF
OF THE BLANTYRE MISSION OF THE
CHURCH OF SCOTLAND

IN GRATEFUL ACKNOWLEDGMENT OF LOYAL
AND AFFECTIONATE FRIENDSHIP THROUGH
MANY YEARS, THIS VOLUME IS DEDICATED BY

THE AUTHOR

PREFACE

IN the following lectures the scope of the term "African" is limited to the peoples living round the south end of Lake Nyasa, on the hills to its west and east, and along the valley of the Lower Shiré River—the Nyanjas and the Yaos. They belong to the race now termed Bantu—a word which, in this or other similar forms in use among these peoples, means "the people." This plural has now been adopted as the general term for these tribes by whom this group of languages is spoken.

Some hundreds of years ago the Bantu swept down from the north, through Central Africa, driving before them the Hottentot and the Bushman, and settled all over Central and South Africa. They were found by the white man broken up into various tribes who appear in history as Zulu, Matabili, Bechuana, etc., south of the Zambezi; and Swahili, Yao, Nyanja, Ngoni, Wemba, etc., north of that river. In language closely akin, they differ but little from each other in beliefs, habits, and customs. Most of what is said regarding the two tribes mentioned above may be taken as largely typical of the faith of the whole Bantu race.

Those who desire fuller and more minute information regarding this race will find it in two works dealing with two Bantu tribes, *The Life of a South African Tribe*, by M. Junod ; and *The Ila-Speaking People of Central Africa*, by Smith and Dale.

CONTENTS

LECTURE I

Native Mentality and Environment

LECTURE II

Native Beliefs

LECTURE III

Shadows and Fears

LECTURE IV

The Appeal through Native Beliefs

LECTURE V

How the Seed is best sown

LECTURE VI

Problems to be faced

THE GOSPEL AND THE AFRICAN

LECTURE I

Native Mentality and Environment

EIGHT-and-forty years ago, in the company of the late Professor Henry Drummond, I was making a brief tour, through the country lying to the east of Blantyre in the Shiré Highlands of Nyasaland. Accompanied by our gang of native carriers bearing our travelling equipment, we were crossing the wide plain that lies between Mounts Mlanje and Zomba. Our path followed a native track through the stubble of the newly burnt grass, that covered a treeless and waterless tract of country. It was almost noonday in month of August, the beginning of the hot season in that latitude. The hot sun, smiting us with its stabbing rays, made us long for the shade of the forest trees that appeared some distance ahead of us along the base of Mount Zomba, which was the goal of our march for the day. We were walking African fashion, in single file. In front of us tramped a burly native porter, bearing his load of fifty pounds, handling it as if it were little heavier than a football, now resting it on one shoulder, now lifting it on to the other, now raising it on to the grass pad he carried on his head to protect his skull from the hard surface of his wooden burden. All the while he sang, and danced from foot to foot, keeping time with his song, and stopping, every now and then, to give his burden a friendly tap with the butt end of the shaft of the short spear he carried in his right hand. Sinewy and lithe in his every movement and gesture, he gaily moved ahead of us while the perspiration poured from head and shoulders in trickling beads over chest and arms. Happy and carefree he appeared to us as he tramped along singing his chant in a sustained monotone for mile after mile through that hot August noonday. Stopping for a moment in his march, Drummond turned to me and said: "I would give all I possess to get inside that fellow for just half an hour."

For five-and-forty years thereafter I was trying to "get inside" and understand such African "fellows" as he, and at the end of all my endeavours I had oftentimes to confess myself almost as much outside them as Drummond and I were outside that " fellow " those many years ago.

To think as an African thinks, " thinking black," as it has facetiously been called—is an achievement impossible to me as a white man. The black man's whole upbringing, environment, and outlook, have raised a high wall between his mind and mine, that I have never got over—a wall built by generations of heredity in an atmosphere vastly different from mine. This difference shows itself in a mentality ruled by influences and motives and powers that have no place in my logic of cause and effect. The African is moved and swayed by unseen and mystic influences that have no place in the white man's process of reasoning, and the path through his field of thought is one impossible for the white man to follow. The African lives in a world full of mystic potencies, and surrounded ever by unseen agencies of a world of spirit powers between whom and himself there is close and constant intercommunion, and which profoundly affect his motives and actions. He lives in a world in which every object is charged with mystic properties, that act and react on one another, and that may, at any moment, be brought into action for or against himself. Mary Kingsley's[1] words written regarding the Negro of West Africa, apply with equal truth to the Bantu of East and Central Africa. "You must always remember that the African mind does not run on identical lines with the European. What may be self-evident to you is not so to him, and *vice versa*. I have frequently heard African metaphysicians say that white men make great jumps in their thought courses, and do not follow an idea step by step as the negro does."

I should use almost precisely the same language in any estimate of the thought processes of the Central African. There appear gaps in his course of reasoning which I cannot get over, but which are filled in by him with unseen and mystic forces and fears that are to him as real as the outer material world with its laws of cause and effect is to me. I believe that from this source he fills in the middle premise which throws awry my examination of his syllogism. It is just this mystic middle premise of which the white man is ignorant, and so believes it wanting, that makes the black man's reasoning so incomprehensible to the white, and which explains the latter's failure to grasp or understand the ground or cause for the former's

[1] Mary Kingsley's *Travels in West Africa*, p. 424.

attitude. I have many a time put before a native of even superior intelligence a course or action such as would undoubtedly be to his advantage, only to find it rejected. Influences were at work in his mind, some fear, some dread of evil that might arise should he rouse the mystic potencies that surround him, to take action against him, the responsibilities of class membership, some taboo that lay across the path I held up to him. These or any of these were at work in his mind and made him turn away from what, to my mind, was to his own best interests. All my arguments had no effect. They fell on ears closed by agencies real to him but unknown to me. Thus each of us living in a world of thought and feeling and prepossession peculiarly his own, made it as impossible for me to understand his attitude to my proposal, as it would have been for Drummond "to get inside" the "fellow" who danced and pranced before us so light-heartedly on that Mlanje-Zomba road these many years ago.

What I have got to say, therefore, in these lectures, is said from my own side of the wall that separates me from the African, where I see things from the spectator's point of view—all I have ever been able to attain to. Any right or reliable interpretation or exposition of the African's outlook on the world must come from the African himself when the time comes for him to sit down and tell us what were the motives that prompted him to action so manifestly counter to his own interest.

I must further say, that in the course of these lectures I shall refer largely to my own experience of two tribes in close association with whom I have passed all the years of my life in Africa—the Nyanja tribe, who live along the valley of the Shiré River and on the lands to the south and south-west of Lake Nyasa, and the Yao tribe, who inhabit the country round Blantyre and Mount Zomba, and to the east and south-east of Lake Nyasa. These two tribes belong to the great Bantu race of Central, East, and South Africa, and differ but little from each other in character, habits, and customs; while both, in their mental and spiritual outlook, may be considered as typical of the Bantu race to which they belong. Any few references I may make to other peoples or other authorities will be for the purpose of elucidating or illustrating from others' experiences what I have learned from my own experience of the two tribes I have mentioned.

Keeping in view therefore, the difficulty that an outsider has in getting at the real nature of the African's outlook on life ; keeping in view also the limited character of the field whose boundaries I have laid down for myself, and believing that in Christianity we have a clear and full response to every need of the heathen soul which by his present religious faith and practice he seeks to satisfy, I purpose, in these lectures, to survey some of the main elements in the African character and the influences that move him to action, and then to find in Christianity the response which will satisfy those needs of the African's soul, which his present beliefs and practices disclose.

With this preface and apology I return to Drummond's "fellow" dancing joyously in front of us as we trudged along the narrow sunbaked path in the direction of Mount Zomba that hot August noonday.

We had picked this man up and added him to our list of carriers, as we passed four days before through a village a half day's march from Blantyre. There one of our carriers had learned of the death of a relation who had lived some miles distant from his home, and he must needs go and attend the funeral rites. Load or no load, journey or no journey, he could go no further with us, and without further parley he made off for his home. However, as we were recognised at the village as hailing from the Mission at Blantyre, we had no difficulty in finding another man to take up the forsaken load, so we enrolled him in the defaulter's place. In a trice, the new man, having seen his name entered on the roll of porters, rushed off home, and speedily returned with a spear in one hand, and in the other a large chunk of cassava root which would serve for his day's ration till he reached camp in the evening. There he knew he would share his meals with the other carriers for whom their employers would provide food, after the manner and custom of white man's travel in that part of the country. His load shouldered, he attached himself to the tail of our line of carriers.

His was a history common to many at that time and in that place, and well illustrates the conditions of native life and native society in those early days. He was a Yao tribesman, and had come from the North-East, from the Yao country that lay among the mountains eastward of the south end of Lake Nyasa. His people had been among the number of those migrants with whom, in the early 'sixties of last century, Livingstone and Bishop Mackenzie had fought in defence of their Nyanja protégés who had settled round the newly formed Mission Station of the Universities Mission at Magomero on the Shiré Highlands. Our porter's people had afterwards settled on a spur running out from the south-east side of Chiradzulo Mountain, and within easy reach of its summit, to which they could flee for safety at the first rumour of an Angoni raid on any of the neighbouring villages. The Angoni were a tribe of Zulu origin whose home was on the lofty plateau west and south-west of Lake Nyasa, which, by making yearly raids on their less warlike neighbours, kept them in a constant state of insecurity and nervous fear. It did not take much to start an "Angoni scare" in those early days. A village woman, overhearing a casual conversation between two passing travellers in which was uttered the word "chikopa," a "shield," would at once surmise they were discussing the Angoni, and would thereupon rush off to her village to give warning of the impending raid. The shield was the distinctive arm of Angoni warriors, and to hint at its actual appearance was to strike terror into the hearts of Yao or Nyanja villagers, and cause instant flight to the nearest mountain-top for safety.[1]

[1] I have known the Blantyre Mission suddenly filled with hundreds of women and children, who had fled thither for safety, terrified by an incident such as I have mentioned above.

Our new carrier's village was a typical Yao village of the time. His home was the usual grass and mud hut that housed his few possessions during the day, and himself, his wife and younger children during the night. The day had begun as every African day had begun for generations on generations. The cock-crow that marks its beginning had roused a few sleepers, and the murmur of early voices came forth from various huts round the village courtyard. Gradually these would increase in number and the whole village awake into life. By and by the creaking of the door of the chief's hut as it was drawn aside between the side posts would give notice of the appearance of the head of the village, who would issue forth, stretch himself, with uplifted arms, and utter a loud " Howa ! " This brought other awakened sleepers from their huts into the open. The male portion of the community would one by one gather in the village courtyard, where amid the ashes of last night's fire some one would blow into flame a bunch of dry grass plucked from some abandoned hut, and round it, crouching over it to warm their hands and bodies, the male portion of the village people would sit, men and boys together. Talk would go on in subdued tones, but loud enough to reach others awake in neighbouring huts and bring them to join the circle round the cheery blaze. By and by, as the glare of sunrise in the east grew brighter, the stillness of the morning would be broken by the now thoroughly awakened poultry, the barking of the dogs, the bleating of the sheep or goats, as well as the voices of the women and children issuing from other huts, until the bursting of the sun from behind the distant Lomwe hills brought the whole village life into the open. Soon with the increasing warmth drying the dew off the grass, the women, each seizing a hoe and axe from her hut, with her baby still asleep on her back tied in his mother's loin cloth, and accompanied by her little boys and daughters, would march off to their gardens down on the plain. The older boys would join their seniors round the courtyard fire, listen for a little to the village gossip or news from the chief's village of the day before, then set off to join their mothers in the fields, or with their fellows organise a hunt after mice and rats in the neighbouring bush or forest. Some of the men would still linger round the village fire, engaged in various occupations, basket weaving, mat making, shaping hoe and axe handles ; while others would march off to the chief's village to listen to some case or lawsuit, in which they might have an interest.

And so the day wears on. By and by the women return from their work in the gardens, each bearing on her head a bundle of firewood, which she had cut on the way home. The girls are sent to the well or stream for water, while the thud, thud of the pestiles in the mortars betoken preparations for a meal—the main meal—sometimes the only real meal of the day. The men gather home, and take up their places round the village fire. There they await their spouses to bring them their food in basket and bowl or plate. They and the boys eat their evening meal by themselves; the women and girls retire to the hut, where they, too, eat apart. The children and the grown-ups may then gather for a dance in the open courtyard beside the village fire. And this more especially on moonlit nights when, through the sound of their leg rattles and tom-toms may be heard the deep, loud beat of the big drums at the chief's village, where the bang of an occasional gun betokens a large orgy of beer drinking. On special nights, song and dance will go on far into the night or even stretch out into the morning. On other nights the village life will retire early within doors, and, save for the murmur of men's voices from within the headman's hut discussing the events of the day, the chirp of the crickets in the trees, the croaking of the frogs in the marsh, the barking of a jackal from a neighbouring thicket, or the chattering of a troop of monkeys disturbed in their slumber by the restlessness of one of their number troubled by dreams, the village community is steeped in silence. And so the days pass as every day has passed all through the years of the life of Drummond's envied carrier.

The changing seasons relieve the monotony of his life—to us monotonous, but to him not without interest and variety. The coming of the rainy season demands the full energies of himself and his family in preparation for and sowing the season's food crop. The rains and the warm sun cause him to fight tooth and nail to keep down the weeds, and give his food crops room and air to grow. For the four or five months of the rainy season, he must devote to this task the whole strength of himself and his family. The dry season, on the other hand, gives him time for repairing his hut or building a new one, or for a journey to the coast with a trading caravan—in the old days with a company of slaves to be marketed at some of the slaving towns on or near the trade routes. In later days he will engage for three months' work with a neighbouring planter, leaving his wife and family to make preparations in the gardens, new and old, for the sowing of next season's crop. And so the months pass.

The monotony of village life is further broken by the recurrent saturnalia of the village initiation ceremony, when the whole village life, male and female, youth, manhood, and age, is moved to violent excitement. The women revel in these times of dissipation, for then are the great times of feast-making and brewing of unlimited cauldrons of beer; while the seniors among them take their part as instructresses of maidens and expectant mothers in the mysteries of womanhood, wifeship, and mothercraft. The old men, grey with the wisdom of years, have their chief place as instructors of youth on the life mysteries of manhood, and initiating them into the knowledge and discipline that will fit them for man's estate and duties. For six weeks or two months these saturnalia last, and the whole village, all that time, seethes with interest and excitement. From these initiation camps the young initiates return to the village to be for a few days the heroes and heroines of the time. Their childhood is ended, their manhood and womanhood is begun. The mysteries of some of life's inmost secrets are theirs now, and a knowledge that fills, with many noxious weeds, soil that God meant for purer plants of grace. The old women and the old men are the repositories and teachers of much of this knowledge, and from them during these days of saturnalia the morality of the village youth takes on its sombre tone.

The close of the harvest season, and the end of the ingathering of the crop, give occasion for the sacrificial feasts of thanksgiving that link his village and community life with the life of spirit that surrounds him all his life from childhood to age. Drought or famine also are factors that disturb the even tenor of village life. In dread of serious loss and privation from either cause, a long procession from the village makes its way to the shrine or grave of some dead chief or headman, where his late subjects deprecate his wrath by sacrifices of food or drink, and plead for his influence in the spirit world to avert the dreaded calamity. No greater evil can come on an African community than a season of famine, when men and women are driven to beg or buy the husks of the grain of their richer neighbours, which in common days they throw to pigs and fowls, or to grub in the forest for roots to cook and save their stomachs from the gnawing pain of emptiness.

Greatest break of all in the monotony of village life is the advent of death in one form or another. In its presence the activities of the village cease, and even the common duties of family life are for a time in abeyance. The village feels itself under the eye of an unseen agency, and in consequence moves softly and suspiciously. No man or woman knows when he may be called to face and defend himself from that most obnoxious crime in African native life—the charge of dealing in the magic spells of witchcraft. The coming of the woman witch finder, sent for when the ordinary diviner fails in his arts to purge the village of the presence of the witch, his charms and medicines, adds to the upheaval of village life on such occasions. Not till the village has been cleared of the witch and his spells will the men and women sleep soundly; and then life will resume its ordinary course, till death again visits the village, and the same awful terror of the witch and his spells resumes its benumbing hold over men's minds and hearts.

The visit of an Arab or coast trader—seeking slaves and ivory—always brought, in the old days, an element of insecurity and uncertainty into village life. Among the Yao tribe very few of the villagers occupied the position of free men—in not a few cases only the actual kith and kin of the headman himself. All others were in some degree or other bound to him in a servitude more or less real, if not in actual slavery. At times of want, which in our own day would be termed "financial depression," or when called on to make payment for damage done by some of his villagers or dependants or fellow-clansmen, or in some way to assist his paramount chief out of his difficulties, the headman would often find an easy way of procuring the necessary finances by disposing of some of these village rascals whom he himself may have acquired in similar circumstances. And at such times woe to the thief or quarrelsome man, or man against whom was the hand of his fellow-men, the idle man, the man who was a source of trouble in the village, the man who for some misdemeanour was confined in a slave stick! Woe to him, for he could readily be disposed of, and the finances of both headman and villagers relieved by the slaver's cloth, or powder, or brass wire, or beads! The presence, too, of the slaver in the district added to the insecurity of village life, for parties of mauraders from neighbouring unfriendly chiefs would prowl about gardens or wells or village bypaths, and woe be to the village maiden or young woman who might fall into their hands!

Actual warfare, a raid by an armed party of Angoni or Makuwa, meant devastation of villages and destruction of crops or grain stores over a wide area. The inhabitants would then flee to the top of the nearest hill, whence from positions of comparative security they would look down on burning huts and plundered grain stores, with the further prospect of months of privation or famine till the next season's crop could be hoed, sown, and reaped. Among the tribes I was familiar with, such raids were of annual or biennial occurrence. The pioneers of Blantyre in 1876 found the people living on the hilltops, only venturing down to cultivate a scrap of garden, on the hill-slopes, or the plain below. The advent of the white man and the white man's rule under British protection changed all that. Said an old woman, "At Blantyre I can sleep in peace now—without dreaming."

Amid such surroundings and breathing such an atmosphere, the African youth grew up—with no moral discipline save his own superstitious fears, no teaching of self-restraint or high ideals of life. The boy especially was free as the air to follow the whims, desires, and promptings of his own sweet will. Save for the household duties which her mother called on her to share, the girl grew up just as Topsy grew up—she "growed." Chastisement of either sex was rarely given, except it were out of loss of temper on the parents' part. "He is my son, not my slave," was the excuse given placidly by a parent who was unmoved by a glaring instance of disobedience to a polite request on the parents' part. "Shan't" was the not unfrequent answer on a boy's part to a father's request prefaced by the soothing prefix "Sir, please!"—an answer received with perfect complaisance by the parent, or even with pride at the son's manliness. "He is not a slave," covered a multitude of disobediences. Only in the ceremonies of the initiation rites was discipline or instruction imparted combined with physical accompaniments, severe at times even to the drawing of blood by the castigations inflicted. Civilised discipline—if I may so apply the adjective to corporal punishment, first came to the lad or girl at school, and there even to this day such is bitterly resented both by pupil and guardian. The very whisper in school or village that the teacher had a cane or strap and used it, was quite enough to empty a school. And it might remain empty for days till the desire for further knowledge overcame their possibly nervous fears of corporal punishment. Yet when given a little authority, whether as teacher or as overseer of a gang of labourers at an industrial task, there is no greater tyrant than the African himself. Among a race grown up in an atmosphere of slavery, when freedom comes, it is apt to be followed by licence, or even cruelty on the part of the newly freed. The old slave is often the worst master, and those responsible for discipline at work or in school have strictly to watch lest any delegation of authority given to a subordinate is not made an excuse for an exercise of discipline that will certainly fail of its end in securing discipline or respect either for teacher or overseer.

But to return to the Native carrier who awakened such interest in Drummond's heart, as he danced before him on the Zomba road, seemingly master of his own life and destiny. General Smuts, the South African statesman, in his Oxford lectures delivered by him in 1929, described the African as the "happiest of mortals." So thought the Dutch General, and so have thought many another who sees the African only from the outside. And so in many ways he is. Every stranger who gets into touch with him marks the light-hearted good humour that is characteristic of the Native in his ordinary daily life. He will meet your kindly greeting with a smile. He will readily respond to humour on the stranger's side. He will accept and readily comply with a request for assistance if made in a half jocular way, which he will resent if given in a less friendly manner. He is susceptible to kindly "chaff," which is always more effective than a cross or harsh reprimand. He is sensitive as to his *amour propre*, and if that is outraged he will relapse into a moodiness that makes him a most uncompanionable companion. He is the politest of mortals, and expects his politeness to be acknowledged. A father's request to his son is generally prefaced by "Please, sir!"[1]

His sense of unity in his clan relationships, limits his responsibilities in one direction and widens them in another. To those outside his brotherhood or clan he owes no debt of any kind, not even the calls of a common humanity. On the other hand, the claims of clanship

[1] Ignorance of this characteristic of the African is a frequent cause of a European's failure to "get on with his native workers." A hectoring, scolding manner never secures prompt obedience or cheerful service. Politeness, even to the humblest of employees, is a trait that the native will understand and appreciate.

involve him in many a task or duty that often runs entirely counter to his own self-interest.

Clanship, which holds so firm a place in his life, follows among the people I am speaking of the line of descent through the mother, and gives character to many of the laws of relationship and marriage and succession of property. The ties that bind him to his mother's family are far closer than those that bind him to his father's relations. His mother's is the ruling influence in his life, and his love for her he never leaves in doubt. To her his heart is always open. In trouble he flees to her, and in pain or anguish of body, the cry on his lips is always "Mother! Mother!" To speak slightingly of his mother is the deadliest of insults. I have known a case of a lad committing suicide as a protest against a disparagement of his mother's honour.

And yet in his boyhood days, his mother's influence had little power. The village lad, promoted from his mother's mat to sleep among his fellows in the common village boys' sleeping-hut or in a hut of his own, soon gains an independence of her affectionate control and goes his own way. The hunt, at first confined to mice and field rats, and small birds, afterwards extended to larger game; the village courtyard and council, with its constant discussion of village social problems; the arguing of cases by the village elders in the headman's or chief's court, draw his attention and interest into other channels, away from his mother. But sickness or mortal pain or bereavement takes him back to his childhood's love, which finds expression in the poignant cry, "Mother! Mother!"

Woman's influence in the settling of family and tribal affairs has no small weight, and in some matters is supreme. The grandmother claims a large share in the ruling of the events of family life. Even under the new régime of civilised custom, in which the husband takes the wife away to his own home, the grandmother—the mother's mother—claims the first-born daughter to replace her lost daughter. "Some one to give me a drink of water," is her argument in support of her claim. Thus it had come to pass, that in the early days of Christianity, when the grandmother was heathen the first-born daughter was in danger of being reared in heathen surroundings. The Church had to legislate in the matter of this growing danger.

Under the rules of clanship, the heir, unless he has already inherited an heirship from another source, is the sister's oldest son who succeeds to both name and position, and takes up the responsibilities and family ties of the deceased uncle.

Clanship rules far more firmly than does family relationship. A clansman is everywhere a brother, though many degrees removed according to our reckoning of kinship. This often tends to callousness or indifference where such relationships and the claims of charity or compassion are concerned. "He is not my brother," is an accepted plea for failure to help where help is asked on another's behalf—and expected. The wider sense of brotherhood and its responsibilities is one of the lessons of Christianity.

The call for clan sympathy or aid is neglected rarely from motives of clan brotherhood, but, in many instances, from fear lest failure to respond, should a fatal issue ensue, lay the refuser open to a charge of witchcraft. On the other hand self interest often vanishes under a sense of the claims of clan brotherhood. I have known good situations thrown up, when to remain meant absence from the bedside of a dying brother, or failure to attend a brother's funeral. I have seen both men and women sit for hours in a crowded hut, and in a cramped position, holding on their knee the head of a sick or dying brother. In similar circumstances the illness of a stranger or non-clansman, would move no single chord of pity.

Loyalty to clan finds its counterpart in loyalty to chief—to chief as chief, apart from personal qualities. The African is able to look past the personal equation, and recognise his duties towards his superior without any appreciation of his moral character. Thus the most foolish, cruel, drunken chief is served with utmost loyalty. It is pathetic to hear the excuses made for such. "He is young"; "He is badly counselled"; "He will be wiser as he grows older." And not a word of criticism or disparagement even in a stranger's ears, although the speaker may easily read disapproval in the stranger's face. And yet when the election of a new chief is made, and when conformity to native law of succession leaves any room for choice, the headmen and the females of the chief's household are very exacting. The virtues and vices of the rival candidates are carefully scrutinised; but when the choice has once been made, all such criticisms are hushed. He is elected with acclamation. He is chief, and unless among the openly rebellious, who are generally very few, the new ruler is accepted with utmost loyalty and served with obedience.

The African has a dumb animal's instinct for character, and a mighty appreciation of goodness, truthfulness, and justice. Although in his ideas of the after-life beyond the grave, character has no effect on the place or state of the soul, yet in this life, character counts for much. In the case of the white man who teaches him or rules him, character counts for everything. Personality is the teachers' and rulers' mightiest weapon of influence, yet he shows this strange seeming inconsistency, that among his fellows with whom he daily associates, he shows no aversion from men who bear a tainted character in the estimation of the community. The known drunkard or thief will always find a place round the village fire, or in the circle about the chief's hut. Whether this characteristic is due to fear of the consequences to himself of any criticism or show of dislike, or whether it is from simple indolence which does not court trouble, it is difficult to say. This, however, may be said with assurance, that the strongest asset a man can take into heathen Africa, whatever his object there may be, is character and the personal influence that accompanies it. Lord Cromer said character counted for 75 per cent. in the influence of a Government official in Africa.

Injustice or cruelty, on the other hand, although resented, is borne with dogged patience and forbearance. It was this power to endure, and great patience that enabled the African race to come through all the years of injustice and slavedom which the treatment of him by the white man caused him to endure, or the miseries he suffered at the hands of tyrants like Lobengula or Chaka. The African has taught the world a lesson of patience and endurance, without which he would never have passed through the cruelties of the Middle Passage, or the atrocities of the early days of the Congo rule, or the injustices of Portuguese rule in their African colonies. Through these he has passed, and reached the dawn of a better day that gives us the hope that in due time his race will take its place on the platform of the world's life, and will bring to the Treasury of God its own gifts of patience and endurance.

Yet the African never forgets an injury or an act of injustice. I have known a wrong cherished in a Native's memory for more than one generation, and only recalled when an opportunity occurred of taking revenge for it. Then he will bring it all back again long after others have forgotten it—and the wrong will be seen to be as fresh in the wronged one's memory as on the day he suffered it.

Much of the limitation that has hemmed him in and stopped his path of progress has arisen from his lack of initiative. He has made little or no progress in any of the arts and crafts of life since the day he first came before the eyes of the outer world. He has made nothing new. He still makes nothing new. He does nothing that his fathers did not do before him. While the great human world outside was gradually, generation after generation, discovering and developing the resources of science and industry, thus enriching its life with its knowledge and skill, the African race stood still. They have gone little beyond the Stone Age which the white man passed through two thousand and more years ago. Stone hammers and stone anvils are still the tools of the blacksmith, and stones are still in use to give weight to their digging pins. Not a nail or scrap of iron goes into their house structure, neither does stone, only grass, wooden poles and bamboos tied together with rope made of the bark of the tree growing on the outskirts of his village. The evidence that the Bantu race ever used anything else is very uncertain.

This lack of initiative has been ascribed to various causes. De Bruhl,[1] an authority on Primitive Mentality, ascribes it to the Natives' belief in the mystic properties and participation of things—a theory which I shall refer to later, and which forbids innovations, " so that one may not have to fear the unknown powers which a fresh form might possess. They make things exactly as their fathers made them. And this not, as we have been told, the result of habit, and of a spirit of conservatism peculiar to these peoples. It is the direct result of active belief in the mystic properties of things, properties connected with their shape and which can be controlled through the shape, but which would be beyond the power of man to regulate, if there were the slightest change of form. The most apparent trifling innovation might lead to danger, liberate forces, and finally bring about the ruin of the instigator and all connected with him."

Another cause of this lack of initiative is the native fear of the suspicion of witchcraft, that a successful innovation would bring on the innovator. This dread hangs ever over the Native. Should his garden be specially productive beyond that of his neighbour's, occult

[1] De Bruhl, *How Natives Think*, pp. 41–42.

means would at once be suspected. The use of fertilisers would be an undeniable evidence and proof of the powers of witchcraft. In fact, prosperity in any kind of occupation, or even skill in any art or craft, gives rise to suspicions that in the end work dire and deadly harm. Central Africa is hemmed in by the past, and unless some new awakening motive power is brought into its life, it will ever remain a stagnant pool.

Another cause of this lack of initiative may be ascribed to the inertia that is produced in the African by the presence in his system of the anchlostome or hookworm, which medical authority tells us infests the bodies of over eighty—some say ninety—per cent. of the native population. This parasite, having its home in the intestinal track, produces an anæmic condition of body, and renders the person listless and without energy. What is often ascribed by the European settler crying out for Native labour, to the "laziness of the Nigger" is largely due to this most insidious of tropical diseases. This disease, acting through generation after generation, cannot have failed to produce a diathesis that would render the Native incapable of thinking out any problem or scheme for self-betterment.

The Native himself aware of this limitation ascribes it to none of these causes, but to the unstable state in which Native society has lived through the long past of his history, and to the constant migration of villagers and tribes to which the Bantu race has been so long addicted, and from whose necessity the recent occupation by the protective powers of Europe has now freed him. Many a Native has replied to me, on drawing his attention to this matter, "Why should I improve my hut, or my village, or my roads from which I may be driven to-morrow? Why should I plant fruit trees for another to eat the fruit thereof?" Apply this reasoning to other possible avenues of native self-improvement, and a strong reason for the stagnation of the African people will be at once apparent.

While the native of Central Africa thus lies under the disability of lack of initiation, his imitative faculty is correspondingly strong in its development. Too strongly in fact, for it militates against any cultivation of the initiative. He will rather copy than invent or develop on his own lines. In clothes, in manners, in social and family customs he will copy the European, and ofttimes makes a very poor copy. In dress the Central African declined the flowing robe adopted by his brethren of the East Coast, preferring the European garb. His womenkind, however, eschewing the example of their sisters in South Africa, have adopted a garment that is admirably suited to native life, and conducive to both modesty and seemliness.[1]

His imitative faculty has led the Native into wonderful reproductions of things he has seen in European use. Bicycles made of bamboos—even the rims of the wheels—without a bit of iron in their construction, chairs and tables carved out of solid blocks of wood or trunks of trees, sun-helmets made of the pith of maize or sorghum stalks, show an adaptiveness that may be a factor in his future life in ways leading to things higher and deeper than the manufacture of bamboo bicycles or pith solar topees.

In common with peoples who do not depend on written records, his memory—especially his locative memory, which he calls oftenest into play—is very acute. Take a native along

[1] This admirable habit is largely due to the teaching of the late Miss Janet Beck, one of the pioneer women missionaries of Blantyre, who led the way in the industrial training of girls and women. She planned a garb admirably suited to the native woman, which in the after years became, and still is, "fashionable" over a wide area in Central Africa.

a road that he may not have traversed for a period of years, and then possibly only once, and he will tell you of every incident on that previous journey; where he rested, where he took a snack of food, where his party made their camp for the night. He will tell you where each branch road leads to, and where a branch road used to exist that has long ago "died," as the native idiom has it. It would almost seem as if he kept a map of the road in his mind—with some note to mark the place of each incident on the way. Add to this an intimate knowledge of natural phenomena, and of the character and habits of the animals in his forests and bush. Add to this again a practical knowledge of the uses to which the products of nature may be applied in his daily wants, illustrating that power of adaptiveness to which I have already alluded, and we again realise how much may be made of this faculty in the future development of the resources of his country.[1]

[1] Instances of this power of adaptiveness are common. From the bark of a tree he makes cloth to form for himself a garment. From the same bark he makes rope to tie his hut together, and twine to make the nets used in hunting. The bark of a tree near a river, stripped and bent canoe shape, he will use to ferry himself and his loads over the river, too deep to be forded on foot. The root of a fibrous plant makes his toothbrush or a sweeping broom. In making a fire on a

This locative memory of his has made him a valuable asset to the industrial development of the country, where a knowledge of machinery is concerned. His recollection of the relative position of the various parts of the engine or machine enables him to become rapidly familiar with their various uses. For many years the steamers on the Zambesi and Shiré Rivers were run by native attendants with only occasional supervision by the white engineer in charge. And now in Nyasaland the natives are taking rapidly to the use and driving of cycles and motor cars, while at the same time some of them are being employed in the engineering workshops of the Central African Railways, and in due course will be driving its railway trains.

In all these matters that come under his own daily observation, the sequence and character of natural phenomena as they pass before him, and the uses to which the products of nature may be put, the native is in himself a mine of information which, on occasion, he can make use of. But of the "whys" and "wherefores" of it all he knows nothing. He

wet night in the bush without a live cinder or flint and steel or matches, his skill amounts almost to genius. Every African lad is a born Boy Scout.

reasons nothing out to its natural conclusion. Pushed for an explanation he answers, "It's just God." And that for him is enough.

Among a people, the hero of whose folk-lore is the rabbit, that lives on the cleverness of the tricks it plays on other and duller animals, and whose deeds are the glory and admiration of youth listening round the camp-fire to wonderful tales of the rabbit's prowess, it is not to be marvelled at if strict truthfulness is not a strong characteristic amongst them. In their mother tongue their word for "clever" has almost always a sinister significance. A lack of imagination, as well as a failure to realise in the future the results of a falsehood, makes lying easy to these African peoples. The consequences of an untruth never, therefore, put any check on the stream of their promises. The natural desire to please gives rein to much untruth. The white man soon learns this to his cost when he begins to ask for information. The answer he will get is the answer which the Native sees will be agreeable to the questioner. To the tired traveller anxious as to the distance of his destination, the answer will be: "Yes, it is near, very near," when it is really miles and miles away. On the other hand, the tired carrier, standing by the stream he has just crossed and asked as to the distance of the next source of water supply suitable for a camping place, will answer his employer: "Oh no, it is very far away, miles and miles." Next morning the head of the party finds himself at a beautiful water pool, after only a mile's march. Conscience puts no embargo for conscience is not yet awake, and the native religious faith carries no reproach for moral fault or failure. The Native is happy if he gains his own end—proud like the rabbit of the cleverness which has helped him to gain it.

Honour lies lightly on the native soul. "Honest injun?" to a lad will evoke, "Yes, indeed it is so," when it is far from being so—an answer coming pat from an unfaltering tongue and a steady eye looking you in the face. After many a disappointment, in the latter years of my African service, I ceased to put any lad "on his honour" lest I should add another stain to the many he already has on his soul.

Fatalism, the "kismet" of the Arab, is a trait that stands out prominent in native character. This fatalism of his—an asset indeed where his surroundings give him so little certainty in his outlook on life—enables him to meet misfortune, accident, or even death, without fear or flinching. I have stood by many death-beds in Africa, and I never have stood by one where the end was not faced without equanimity or even indifference. It may be that the disease was due to climatic elements that benumbed consciousness or dulled sensibility as to the future. I rather believe that this attitude is just part of that characteristic of fatalism which helps him over so many rough places in his life.

Closely allied to this fatalism is that insensibility to physical pain which the Native displays —a characteristic that every stranger remarks. One has seen a carrier strike his toe on a stump or stone on the path with such force as to wrench off the toe nail, leaving it attached only by a tag of skin and flesh. He will stop, lay down his load, take his knife from his belt, cut through the tag, throw the nail away, tie up the bleeding toe with a piece of rag torn from his loin cloth, replace his knife in its sheath, snatch up his load, and run limping after his fellows without so much as a wince on his face. This physical insensibility to pain may be just a phase of that dullness of sense and sensation that enables him to face misfortune or calamity, as well as physical suffering, with an equability of temper to which the civilised man is a stranger. Where the alleviations of science or medical skill are awanting, this lack of fine sensibility may be meant to fill a place in the economy of Nature's mercifulness. We pay a big price for the high-strung condition into which the strain of our modern civilised life has brought us.

Closely allied to this fatalism and insensibility to physical pain is the attitude of hopelessness in the face of critical times in his life, which to every onlooker is very apparent. Notwithstanding his usually bright, cheery nature, there are times when he seems utterly overwhelmed by fates which he believes to be against him. In the case of bereavement this is specially to be noted. No one who has ever listened to the wail of an African woman over her dead, but must have realised something of the blank which the lack of Christian comfort leaves in her soul. The saddest sound in all Africa is that of the *maliro*, "mourning"—the wail of the village women as it rises suddenly through the stillness of an African night. To me that wail for the dead has always seemed the most poignant call for the Gospel that comes out of the heart of Africa. It is St.

Paul's vision in a new form of the Man of Macedonia, "Come over and help us." To that call, as to much else that lies in the African soul, the Christian Gospel gives the fullest—the only answer.

LECTURE II

NATIVE BELIEFS

IN my last lecture I dealt with the surroundings, the character, and some of the most outstanding features of the disposition of the Central African tribesman as typified in the carrier whom Drummond and I saw dancing before us on the Mlanje-Zomba road that hot August noontide. To the eye of the onlooker he seemed the light-hearted, care-free soul whom General Smuts described as the " happiest of mortals," thinking of nothing but the joy of life and its material satisfaction. And indeed to every stranger he bears this character. But there's another side—a side revealed by various signs and marks he bears on that stalwart body of his. Those cicatrices seen on chest or limbs are the scars of cuts into his flesh made by his medicine-man as he rubbed in the herbs which have properties that will heal or prevent one or other of the many ailments he may have been at any time addicted.

Round his forearm is tied a pad of red cloth filled with the ashes of some medicinal substance the village "doctor" has given him as a protection against illness on his travels or to save him from danger of such wild animals as he might meet with. Round his ankles are bound anklets of beads alternating with tiny pieces of the rootlets of some plant that will save him from the aches and pains associated with the fatigues of travel. Round the shaft of his short spear is tied the charm that will make it a more serviceable weapon if called into use for attack or defence. These various medicines or charms have their potency, not from any virtue in themselves, but from some mystic power or influence they bear with them. They are the signs or vehicles of realities that are not of the earth earthy, but which have their source in that world of spirit and spirit influence, amid which the native ever lives and moves. He is no materialist—far from it. The things that move him most are not the things that are seen, but the things that are unseen. It is of these unseen mystical powers and influence that I am now to speak of in this lecture to-day. They have been called by various names, "fetish," or "fetichism," "animism," "dynamism," "community of essence," "mystic participation," "mana." Though the names vary with the authorities who employ them, they agree in this, that they refer to realities which belong to the region of spirit and partake of the nature of spirit. Their origin lies in another world from that in which humanity lives, and they are the real, the ultimate and controlling motives and agencies in human life.

These mystic powers, agencies, or influences operate in two relations—there are those that are related to things impersonal and inanimate, and there are those that are related to things personal and animate. Both partake of the nature of spirit. The application of the word "spirit" to the mystic qualities that are in things animate and personal is easily understood, and I shall speak of it later. Its application to the mystic element in things inanimate or impersonal is more difficult to understand, because we associate the idea of spirit so much with things living and personal. As applied to things material and inanimate, the African has no name for it—and can give us no description of it, but it may be defined as that "mystic essence or influence by which one material object or entity operates on another."

Edwin Smith, the author of *The Golden Stool*, calls it by the name of "Dynamism," and defines it as " an all-pervading force which all men conceived of before they came to believe in spirit or God." De Bruhl describes it under the name of the " law of participation," according to which one object, event, or phenomenon " participates " in the nature properties and life of that of which it is the image.[1] The exact nature of this mystic force or influence no writer has yet defined, but we know it is of the nature of spirit, and, therefore, the term " spirit " may be applied to it, as being in things inanimate closely allied to the idea of spirit in things animate and personal.

To the African, therefore, every object in nature has its " spirit," its mystical essence, its motive power in the " law of participation," its " dynamism," and it is through this spirit that one material object acts on another. Hence the origin of that so-called " sympathetic magic " or " homeopathic magic " by which a part of an object may influence or act on the whole. Hence the attempt of the ill-wisher to obtain some part of his victim's person—hair, nail, or even clothing worn on the body—through whose spirit an influence may be brought to bear on the spirit of the person

[1] The Melanesian gives this impersonal essence or potency the name of *mana*.

himself. Hence, too, the wearing of charms and amulets about the person, that the power of the charm, through its spirit, may act on the spirit of the wearer. This explains the confusion that arises from the native use of the term "medicine" which he applies equally to the "drug" of the chemist and doctor, and to the charms he receives from his medicine man, and wears about his person. Hence the wearing of the small pad of the ash of some medicinal plant, first burnt that the spirit in it may more readily reach the spirit of the disease it is meant to cure. The same end is sought by decocting the medicinal plant and giving it to the patient to drink, that in this way its spirit action may more readily and directly attack the spirit of the ailment. The native medical practitioner does not distinguish between the chemical or therapeutical effect of the decocted root, and the effect of the same worn as a twig round wrist or ankle. The term "medicine" is equally applied to both. They are in use all through life from the "medicine" or "charm" tied round the wrist of the infant by a mother anxious to protect her progeny from every possible enemy to its young life, to the similar twig tied round the ankles of the old man on whom the frailties of age are felt in aching limbs and feeble footsteps. The hunter never goes off on the chase without his "medicines" wrapped up in an old rag twisted round the stock of his gun or the shaft of his bow.

The spirit in the medicine or charm acts on the spirit of the weapon and ensures accuracy of aim. Should he by any chance fail to bring down his quarry, it is not because of any failure of skill on his part, but because of the more powerful medicine employed by some rival hunter to render his efforts futile. The gardener or husbandman protects his small crop by hanging horns filled with medicine all round his field-plot—a fence which not the most daring of thieves will venture to get over. The witch applies his power in the shape of horns filled with medicines which he buries in the verandah or secrets in the grass of the roof of the hut of his victim. The potency of all these forms of mystic influence is due to the spirit that lies within the agent used.

Even acts have a mystic or magical influence that goes far beyond their direct action so that the deeds of one individual in a community may affect the life of a whole village. One man's breach of a village taboo may thus work dire misfortune on the entire community. A husband living away from his home, even at the distance of the mines in South Africa, may, by a breach of marital chastity, cause serious disease to attack his wife, living on the shores of Lake Nyasa, two thousand miles away. Similarly a wife who has been unfaithful in her husband's absence, does not put salt into her husband's food lest he should be attacked by a serious form of dropsy. She must get a little girl who has not been through the initiation ceremonies to perform this act for her—and in this way she often betrays her guilt to a jealous and watchful husband. There is a certain mystical relation between the actions of individuals and the well-being of the whole community which thus often necessitates the imposition of a taboo on the actions of its members. The headman of the village is hemmed in by a number of such restrictions which condemn him to rigid abstinence on certain occasions, and to a wild orgy of indulgence on others. Such taboos affect the natural processes of nature at spring-time and harvest-time. On the observance or breach of such taboos, the success or failure of the crop depends. Hunting and fishing ventures, the movement of villages or individual houses, trading expeditions to the coast with an ivory or slave caravan, all come under the protection of charms and medicines supplied to the members of the party, and are subject for their success or failure to the observance or breach of taboos imposed on the relatives left in the village at home Family events such as marriage or death are all bound by certain mystic rites—on whose observance the welfare of the members depends. An omission or neglect of the accustomed rites may cause grave misfortune to the whole family life, which is thus bound together in the one bundle of life. St. Paul's adage is true not of Christianity alone, "No man liveth to himself, and no man *dieth* to himself." The demands made on the Native for his presence at the funeral of a relative that he may take part in the rites connected therewith is thus explained.

Many an employer of labour may suddenly find himself sadly inconvenienced by the departure of a gang of labourers called home that they may thus take part in the funeral rites of their headman or chief. Tidings of death or illness in her cook's family may sadly inconvenience the household arrangements of the lady householder who will find herself suddenly deprived of his services. He must, at all costs to himself, attend the sick-bed or the funeral of the uncle or the "little mother" who may after all be only, according to our nomenclature, a very distant relation, if any relation at all. But the cook knows that absence on such an occasion would be held to be a grave breach of filial duty, if it did not finally lay him open to the awful charge of the practice of witchcraft to procure the illness or the death of the relative in question.

We go back, therefore, to the native porter, dancing before us on the Zomba-Mlanje road, and look at him again, and think of him no longer as a being moved only by material interests and motives, with no thought or care beyond those which minister to his bodily wants or self-indulgence. We recognise him now as living in a world ruled by mystic, unseen, and spirit forces, that are to him as real and as potent as those material motives we usually ascribe to him as the reasons for his actions. It is not the material concerns or influences of life that are the main determining factors in his conduct or character. It is those unseen powers emanating from the unseen world of spirit which most largely sway his motives to action in one direction or another.

These unseen, immaterial agencies are the things in life he dreads most, and these are the things he flies to for safety when the waves of fear or misfortune roll over him. Pierce deep enough beneath the careless, happy, thoughtless demeanour of his which that carrier presented to us on the Zomba Road, and we will find that to him, heathen and all as he was, and is, the things that matter are not the things that are seen, but the things that are unseen. All life to him is ruled by forces from the unseen that are entirely beyond his control. In the African laws of sequence there is no such thing as chance. Cause and effect are everywhere the result of mystic forces, that are above and beyond the laws of the material world in which mankind lives. The mystic alone rules and counts. The spirit of matter acts on the spirit of other matter, and produces its own result. That is the African law of all cause and effect. It is a law of spirit influence not of dynamic force.

It is, however, when we come to consider the rule of spirit in the animate and personal world that we find ourselves in a higher—much higher—region of spirit influence. Among the two peoples I am chiefly dealing with, in fact, among the whole Bantu people of Africa, the subject of the individual spirit or souls of men is one of profound interest and concern, and leads the mind of the Native into a far higher region of thought than does the conscious or unconscious working of spirit and spirit influence in the material world, of which I have just been speaking. The Native openly realises and acknowledges the existence of this spirit world in human life. It is the spirit of man which binds life together, that on this side of the grave to that on the other. These lives are not two but one, for the spirit of man which passes out of this world into that beyond binds both together. Living and dead are still one—one life, one community, united in the relationships that are there just what they were here. There is no break—the one passes into the other, and the veil between is thin. The spirit or soul that leaves the body to-day may be communicated with to-morrow by that prayer and sacrifice which enter so largely into the inner life and world of the African, so near do the two worlds come, and so close is the communion of the life here with the life yonder.

I have used the words "spirit" or "soul." Among the peoples of the tribes I am here thinking of, there is no distinction between the two, such as we have in Pauline psychology. Neither among these people is there any diversity of soul conditions or hierarchy of souls such as is found among some of the West African tribes. There is only the one type of soul or spirit which is the source of life, and is that part of human personality which survives after death. Of the spirit or soul there is only the one class—without distinction of character. Character in life has no bearing or effect on the life after death—character does not enter into the Natives' conception of the soul's state hereafter, save in the case of one class of spirits who, as a class, stand out alone, the Ziwanda, or "evil spirits." They bear this evil character in Native eschatology—but why or how they are supposed to have acquired it I have never been able to ascertain. Their recognised property is their "badness"—their "mischievousness," and any human being taken possession of by such a spirit is in a very parlous state. The Native confesses he knows little about them save that there is such a class of spirits, and they are universally looked on with abhorrence.

I have not found it possible to get at the mind of the natives as to the immortality of the soul or spirit. The future life beyond the grave is an article of his religious faith, but how far he rises to the conception of the endlessness of that future life is a matter of doubt. In the languages of the two tribes I am dealing with, there is no word for " eternal "—it can only be rendered by " unending." In the tongue of a neighbouring tribe on the west shore of Lake Nyasa—the Tongas—the missionaries say they have found a word with the distinct meaning of eternal—*muyaya*—a meaning which would seem to be borne out by the onomatopoetic value of the syllables of which the word is composed. Further study of the innermost recesses of the native consciousness may in due course discover in this matter depths in the native mind that have not yet been plumbed.

In this connection, however, it can be said with every certainty that death brings no change in the status or character of the soul as it leaves its earthly tenement and passes into the unseen. As it lived, so it passes into the future life. The chief in this world is still the chief there with all his wants and all his retinue about him; and the slave is still the slave, bound to his master as when on earth. The chief, therefore, requires servants where he has gone, and so in some clans slaves were slain and laid in the grave or were buried alive beside their masters that their spirits might attend to his spirit in the future life. Articles of value he had about him were also laid beside him—

broken or torn that their spirits might be free to accompany their owner. If the dead had been a wealthy man, the destruction of valuable property was often very considerable.

In the last instance of the burial of an old chief near Blantyre nearly fifty years ago—a chief who was in the heyday of his power when Livingstone and Bishop Mackenzie first visited the country, and who, as the head of a people deeply involved in the slave traffic, gave the Universities Mission no small trouble—the influence of the Blantyre Mission was able to prevail on the people to forgo their old practice of slaying or burying alive slaves with the body of the dead chief. During the ceremony of interment, however, after the body had been laid in its place, a slave descended into the grave, and standing astride the corpse, fired into the air an arrow which floated away into the distance and finally fell into the forest some scores of yards away. There it was left. The intent or meaning of this action, or what relation it had to the rite that had that day for the first time been omitted, I was never able to ascertain ; it had never been done before, and I have never heard of it being done since.

The spirit of man is ever associated with his shadow. To trample on the shadow would certainly be said to endanger life, although in actual practice not much heed is given to this precaution. To take away the shadow would be to kill, and hence the Native, in the early days of his association with the white man was nervous about entering a room where pictures were hung on the walls. "Spirits," he would whisper to his neighbours equally unbrave in this daring adventure. The term used by him to describe pictures or photography, is the word that in the language in common use denotes the "shadow." Hence his nervousness in their presence. Hence, too, his early terror of being photographed—that action being described as "taking away the shadow." Damage to photographic plate or film would undoubtedly be attended with disastrous results to the "subject" before the camera.

Once in those early days a chief whose photograph I had been able to persuade him to have taken took gravely ill. The question was at once mooted among his attendants, whether the sickness was due to the photographic plate with the "image" of their chief on it having been broken in Scotland whither they knew I had sent it. An appeal to the diviner's arts set their minds at rest. He told the inquirers that the plate was intact, and the cause of the sickness must be sought elsewhere. The sickness proved fatal, and the usual steps were taken to ascertain the guilty person whose spells had bewitched the chief. The diviner this time found the death due to three persons who were at once accused of the crime. They appealed to the poison ordeal, and in this case, two out of the three succumbed. The third recovered and claimed compensation for "defamation of character," which was awarded him according to native law bearing on such a case.[1]

Between the two worlds on either side of the grave there is close and constant intercommunication. The dead make their presence known (1) by dreams in which the spirit of the departed appears to the living in their sleep. As the African for the most part is abstemious, or fasts altogether for the greater part of the day, but partakes of a heavy meal at night, dreams are frequent and play a great part in the Native's life. Often late at night the missionary will be visited by some inquiring troubled soul, disturbed by visions in his

[1] The common belief recorded by more than one writer, that the natives say a corpse has no shadow, I have never been able to verify. Doubtless the native would say, in this case, that the shadow seen of the corpse on the way to the grave is that of the mat in which the corpse is wrapped.

slumber which he cannot unravel, and concerning the meaning of which the missionary's interpretation and advice are sought. (2) In trances, also, the spirit world is visited from this side, and the visitor on returning to consciousness relates his experiences, which make a great impression on his fellows. (3) Again, the spirit of the dead may return and visit the scenes of its former life in the shape of a wild beast—a lion, a leopard, a snake, or other animal—its place in the graded scale of the animal world corresponding to the rank in society the deceased held when in life. These visitations generally take place near the scene of the deceased's earthly life or about his grave. They are believed to be real incarnations of the dead, and when seen are held as sacred and receive every possible protection. (4) The spirit again may take possession of some person of weaker intellect, who in consequence may become thoroughly insane, and get out of all control. For this cause the "village idiot" is treated with full respect. Such, in their insane state, are designated as "they of the spirits." (5) Under the influence of spirit possession, some individuals fall into a raving condition, and are in that state supposed to give prophetic utterance to which great credence is attached.

This type of spirit possession corresponds closely to the *nabii* or " seer " of the Old Testament.[1]

It is, however, in his approach to the spirit world from this side that this matter of communion between spirit and spirit has most interest for the African. As the dead have still an interest on the lives of those left behind them in this world, it is natural that they should be believed to possess some influence on their fate and fortune. This interest is—strange to say—most usually exhibited and recognised by the living when it appears in the form of some calamity such as famine, pestilence, drought, or floods accompanied by destruction of crops in the fields near the river banks or in the gullies down which in the rainy season overflowing streams rush, carrying all before them. Such calamities are looked upon as manifestations of the anger of some spirit or spirits, roused by neglect of the appropriate deference due to them in the form of sacrificial offerings. The angry one may be the spirit of some dead chief or ancestor, or near relative recently deceased, any or all of whom still

[1] In the matter of dreams of any kind regarding living persons, these are ascribed to visits by the spirit of the living person which in his sleep is free to roam among other persons and cause dreams. And so in like manner, to dream of the living is ascribed to a visit to them by the spirit of the dreamer.

have an interest more or less in the things of earth. That anger must be appeased, and to this end an offering must be made at the fitting place and in a fitting way to the spirit of the offended one.

But it is not alone in the presence of calamity that the dead are supposed to take notice of the living and the living to make remembrance of the dead. The great events of the daily life of family or village community are still related to those who, in the spirit world remember those alive on earth or are by them still remembered. The planting, hoeing, and harvest seasons, a birth, a marriage festivity, a hunt on a large scale, a journey to the coast with slaves or ivory are all events in which the paternal or ancestral spirits are supposed still to have an interest, and in consequence their favourable recognition is sought. A human soul, thus surrounded by and closely linked with denizens of the other world from whom he can never be far separated, cannot be without a desire to get into touch with them. To effect this and to keep this touch is the main religious desire in the African's soul. He seeks to get this touch and to keep this communion by an approach to some individual spirit, some definite being localised at some shrine or place which the dead may be expected to frequent, and where in consequence he may be expected to be found.

The grave where the dead was laid by the living whom he left mourning his loss is therefore the most likely of all places where living and dead can meet. Over the grave therefore a shrine is erected, where prayers may be made and offerings laid. There, too, already were deposited the articles in daily use by the deceased and which he is supposed still to need—the broken spear or bow on the grave of the husband or father or son, the broken pot on the grave of the mother, the torn school-book on the grave of the schoolboy or girl—saddest spectacle of all, for it denotes the end of the old and the beginning of the new. These in due course rot or decay, and piety suggests a renewal of the offering as an act of deprecation or thanksgiving. The hut where the deceased lived is also supposed to be a haunt of the ancestral disembodied spirit. The hut is levelled to the ground, for no one dared venture to sleep in it again ; but the tiny scrap of clothing or rag of cloth waving at the top of the bamboo stuck into the ruins declares, like a miniature flagstaff, the piety of those who in their simple fashion remember the dead. On great days in the village life—a harvest thanksgiving or initiation ceremonial—a special shrine may be erected on the outskirts of the village—a small shed or hut where offerings are laid and prayers made. Chiefs and headmen of note or ancient fame generally have their shrine on some mountain top whither the people, in their time of distress or rejoicing, make their pilgrimage and lay their offerings. On the top of Mount Michiru, a few miles from Blantyre, there is the shrine of a blacksmith chief—marked by a circle of hoes—a token of homage to the craft of the dead man.[1]

On occasions the offering may be made at the foot of the tree in the village courtyard where the deceased used to sit and talk with his fellows, or sometimes at the site of his dismantled hut. If, on a journey, the traveller is prompted for some reason or other to an act of devotion, he may lay his gift at the root of any tree by the wayside. A scrap of food thrown on the ground before commencing to eat a meal as a " grace before meat," is accepted by the spirit in lieu of a larger and more worthy sacrifice.

[1] On the last occasion that I visited this shrine, I found an offering had been newly placed—of hoes, as usual, but *from Birmingham*. Thus the old and the new meet in Central Africa.

The nearest approach to what is called on the West Coast *fetish*, is reached when the spirit of the dead has been located in some object which is thereafter set apart as a "household god," and laid up generally beside the bed of the owner, and to it prayers and offerings are made. This object may be a basket, a gourd cup, or any odd piece of cast-away cloth. Into this the medicine man or local "doctor" entices the spirit and it is thus located, and so rendered easy of approach. One native headman I knew produced a small pill box procured from some mission dispensary, and in this he said the spirit of his predecessor was located. Such things are rarely spoken of, and are never exhibited in public. The object itself is never worshipped—worship is given to the spirit of the deceased thus located. Occasionally the spirit of an important chief may be enshrined in an animal as a goat or a fowl. The spirit of Chikuse, a late chief of the Southern Angone tribe, was thus localised in a heifer which was thenceforth recognised as sacred, and was always brought on the scene when an offering was made to the spirit of the dead chief. When the animal died, the habitant spirit was transferred to another animal.

The offerings as a rule consist of food.

Beer is the most common article offered. It is poured into a pot or gourd cup, set on the grave, or at the shrine. Through a hole in the bottom the beer trickles and soaks into the ground. Sometimes a reed is inserted in the grave when it is filled in, and thus the liquid reaches the mouth of the corpse. Among the two tribes I am chiefly thinking of in these lectures, flesh is rarely offered—possibly because neither is a pastoral tribe. Nor is blood considered a vital element in any offering of food. Part of the offering is presented to the spirit, the rest is consumed by the worshippers present as a sacrificial feast. Thus communion with the spirit of the dead is sought and obtained in the common sacrificial meal. Just as in life they sat round the one food plate or shared in the one beer pot, so still they sit as it were in each others presence, and partake of the same food in an act of fellowship and friendship.

The offering is left at the grave or shrine, but the spirit partakes of the essence or spirit of it. Even though vermin or ants devour the material of it, the spirit has already accepted and partaken of the gift offered.

The offering of the sacrifice is accompanied by devotions. These consist of thanksgiving and supplication offered by the officiating priest

—to which the rest of the worshippers respond with chant or song. Action or gesture is as natural to an African as speech, and his feelings are oftentimes expressed in actions of a striking dramatic type. The clapping of hands, the swinging of the body in contortions that count for gracefulness in the eye of the Native, the peculiar "ululation" that only an African woman can produce, and even dancing are all methods and vehicles of praise. It has been wittily said that "Songs of war and other sad occasions are the only ones that are not sung with the feet." But among the Angoni, a tribe akin to those I have mentioned, even the songs of war are accompanied by that loud stamping of the feet that seemed to shake the ground with the intent to encourage the warriors' own hearts and strike terror into the hearts of the enemy.

Do we Scots missionaries do right by our converts in imposing on them our own quiet, solemn, and expressionless form of worship? With us the officiating minister almost alone voices the devotion of the worshippers in audible expression—leaving to the congregation only the hymns and psalms. These, after all, form but a small part of the service of worship. While the native on occasion will sit dumb and still for hours in wonderful silence, yet he loves action, loves to demonstrate his feelings in an outward appearance of things. At feast or festival he will deck himself in showy, sometimes fantastic garb ; at funerals he will put on his shabbiest garments—going back at times to his primitive bark cloth. Such things are accepted by him as a suitable expression of his feelings—joy or grief, as the case may be. Have we, Scots folk, by the sombreness of our forms of worship which we have imposed on him, given the African an equivalent for that visible and physical expression of his feelings which his old form of religious worship afforded him ? On this subject, as on so many others that the would-be reformer of the African peoples is faced with every day, the African himself will in his own time give his own opinions in his own way.

Among our Nyasaland peoples there is no priestly class or professional priesthood to lead their worship. The officiant, on the occasion of any communal ceremony or celebration, is usually the most important personage in the community—one who from position or relationship with the spirit to be worshipped might be supposed to have influence with its object. A near relative or fellow-clansman of standing would naturally be expected to possess such influence and thus take the office of priest on such occasion. I have known a member of a conquered and almost enslaved tribe chosen to be the officiating priest on the occasion of a community celebration, by reason of his being a close connection by descent from the conquered chief of the country whose anger was supposed to be the cause of the drought that had visited the district. He would thus be more likely to have influence on such an occasion than a member of the conquering tribe.

In this instance of which I am speaking, when the chief of the conquering tribe died at a very advanced age and much feared by his people, the community worship, hitherto given to the spirit of the old conquered chief of the country, was transferred to the spirit of the recently deceased conqueror, and the old original chief will soon be entirely forgotten.

There are among districts round Blantyre more than one such shrine, at which worship is paid to the spirits of chiefs and headmen long deceased. In ancient days, when chiefs, as we know, had rule over far wider areas of territory than those of later times, their graves became shrines to which people flocked from a distance, and hence their name and repute extended over a wide area far beyond the limits of their original domains. Their memory was cherished in the minds of the people and reached a sanctity lasting for generations. Their ascendancy gradually increased, until they were accorded a place in the hierarchy of the unseen far above that of their fellows, and until, in some cases, they were accorded attributes that were very little remote from divine.

Such beliefs in the continued existence of the human soul or spirit after death, and the practice of the worship of that spirit by the living, are almost universal among the Bantu tribes of Central Africa, and constitute the fundamental factor in their religious outlook. When we pass beyond this primitive faith and practice and consider the question of the evidence of faith in a Spirit higher than that of a dead chief or ancestor, we find ourselves in a region largely of conjecture. Does their faith in the after-life and the worship of the ancestral spirit allow room for faith in the existence of a Supreme Being, ruling over all spirit beings, and does it attach to Him the attribute of personality? In other words, may the messenger of the Gospel approach the people whom he is sent to evangelise, justified in appealing to them as already believing in a Personal God, who is Spirit, and Creator, and Ruler of all things?

Looking over the whole field of Bantu theology, we find there are in different parts of Central Africa names attached to spiritual beings to which we seem compelled to attach the attributes of Personality and of Deity. There are several of those names prominent in Bantu religious thought. Among the Zulus in South Africa there is one whose name, "Unkulunkulu," literally translated, means the "Great-great-One," and thus seems to refer to some very far back ancestor of wide fame, or to one in the spirit world supreme to all the others. Another name in similar use signifies the "Sky," and may be used to signify the Deity, much as we use the word "Heaven." Says Edwin Smith,[1] the joint author of a remarkable book on *The Ila-Speaking Peoples of Central Africa*, "We reach the conclusion that the South African tribes have a conception of God; they are aware of Him, but have no personal name for Him; they approach Him in prayer, but only on great occasions. The ancestors occupy the centre of their field of

[1] Smith, *The Secret of the African*, p. 89.

vision, the Supreme Being has been thrust to the circumference, and is but little regarded."

On the West Coast and up the Congo, we have "Nyambi," occupying this significant central position in the worship of the people. In West Central Africa we have "Leza," which from its derivation signifies "Creator" or "Nurse." In Central and East Africa we find the term "Mulungu," with its variants "Mluku" and "Muungu." This is the word which the missionaries working among the tribes of that region have adopted to designate the Supreme Being. Among the Atonga and Atumbuka, two tribes amongst whom the Livingstonia Mission of the Church of Scotland is working, a word is used, "Chiuta." Etymologically this means the "Big Bow," which would seem to bring it into some relation with the Rainbow, which is known locally as the "Bow of Leza" —the "Bow of God." One missionary among the Atonga tribe on the west shore of Lake Nyasa tells me that prayers are never offered to "God" direct, but only through some ancestral spirit, who is asked to plead with "God" for them. This is contrary to the usage of the neighbouring tribes, who approach the Deity direct.

The word "Mulungu," used by the tribes

we have been principally thinking of, is used with various significances. (1) It is applied to the spirit of an individual in substitute for the more common term "msimu." (2) It is applied to anything connected with God Himself, Divine Worship, the Church Building, the Bible, the Minister's Robes, the Church Bell, etc. These are described by the heathen as "Mulungu"—uttered in an awed whisper. (3) Seeing the white man's week begins on Sunday—a day connected with the worship of God—the people round Blantyre call the week itself by the same divine term. (4) It is also used to signity "fate," or "fortune"—good or ill. In fact, anything that is unusual or inexplicable and whose origin cannot be accounted for is "God." (5) To worship any spirit of the dead is "to worship God." The word, therefore, has reference to what is unseen, inexplicable, and linked with the spirit world.

On the other hand, we note that this word etymologically carries with it no idea of personality. It belongs to that class of nominatives which denote qualities or attributes—things conceived in the abstract. It is never either grammatically or in common speech associated with personality. Once, after trying to explain to an unusually intelligent native headman the Christian idea of the Personality of God, I was astonished to hear him commence speaking of " Mr. God," using the term of respect when speaking of or to a person. Evidently for the first time, God had been thought of in terms of personality, and so the term " Mr. " was used out of respect. On the other hand, when the Native uses the phrase descriptive of death as " going to God " —a phrase very common and touching in use— the preposition used is that of simple locality, not of personality.

Taking the whole subject into view, both from a grammatical as well as a theological point of view, there is, I think, but one conclusion, that the people we have been thinking of do not in any way associate the idea of personality with their conception of God. In their minds, " God " would appear to be the " Spirit World in General," or the " aggregate of all the spirits of the dead," and it is this conception of spirit-thought of either individually or in the aggregate, that constitutes in the native mind the idea of God, and which is worshipped as God. God is with them the disposer of their destiny. " It is God," is the statement constantly on the native lips in the presence of fortune, good or bad. He—I use the personal pronoun—is an intense reality to them. He is with them all through life, and to Him they go at death. The early missionaries were happy in finding, ready as it were to hand, this word which they could use in application to the Christian God of Whom their Evangel spake. It was ready to form a foundation on which the preacher of the Gospel could build the fabric of its faith in the soul of the men and women whom he was sent to seek and to save. The seed of the Evangel thus finds soil, ready prepared, for the seed he is to sow.

Under the consciousness of such a spirit world, filled with spirit life all about him, we find our Native, light-hearted and seemingly care-free as Drummond's "fellow" was, with an ever-present sense of unseen mystic powers and influences about him. Walking through the forest, he may hear a twig snap and fall, and at once start to attention. "There's a spirit there." His devotion calls him to answer by throwing a tiny piece of twig broken from the nearest branch, toward the direction whence the sound came—a "gesture," to use a newly coined expression, that stands for a more worthy offering, thus promised in due course.

He will hear, amid the thicket, the drums of the spirits beating for the dance. Even in his sleep, the spirits will come and whisper dreams into his ear, dreams he will ponder when awake and ask his wiser friends to interpret for him. Far from being a materialist, the largest and most powerful realities in his life are those of the spirit. The Bantu world is therefore full of the things that are spirit—a world surely in which the Gospel that deals with things spiritual and eternal will find a ready home.

LECTURE III

Shadows and Fears

OF the many elements that touch the mind and heart of the African Native, of whom we have been speaking, none is more potent or casts a darker shadow over his whole life than the element of fear. It surrounds him on every side. It may arise from the secret influences and powers of the other world, or its origin may be in the machinations of his earthly enemies. Were it not for the fatalistic stoicism that forms so prominent a trait in his character, and which enables him to hold up his head with a smiling face against the most hopeless of evils that are befalling him, this hydra-headed monster of fear would undoubtedly devour him. He looks Fate in the face, and accepts it as it comes, "It's just God." That is enough. I have met a native on the path, stopped and chatted with him, and joked with him, and he with me, till we parted with a kindly smiling "Good-night."

It was not till next day that I learned he was on his way to the grass shed in the bush where he had been ordered to drink, next day, the poison ordeal to clear himself from an accusation of witchcraft. Doubtless his faith in the never-failing accuracy of the ordeal kept the smile on his face as he went on to meet the morrow; but in this case his confidence was misplaced, for he died as a result of the test. Marvellous was his indifference, and that of many doomed to pass through like ordeals, yet when we turn to look at the many means by which he seeks to avert the forces he dreads, and the pains he takes to defeat them, we can then understand how heavily the fear of them lies on him, and makes him fly to any means that will assure him of safety.

The drought or famine or pestilence or rainstorm may be the action of some ancestral spirit whom he may have unwittingly offended by neglect of his due offerings at grave or shrine. But which spirit has he offended? To whom must his propitiatory offering be made? His own immediate ancestors, who are deeming themselves forgotten? or some predecessor in office of chief or headman? Or mayhap—and this is a not unfrequent source of the severer ills of drought or pestilence

—it may be the anger of some chief of long ago who was deposed from his power and overlordship by a war of conquest, and who now in this way seeks to remind those who hold his place of their duty to the shade of him into whose heritage they have violently thrust themselves. He knows that no native forgets an injury—even after the lapse of many years, an old grudge or quarrel may break out ; and this law of revenge runs into the other world as well as right through this.

The magic spells of his enemies and ill-wishers cause him only to seek more powerful spells by which to circumvent them. He protects his house by "horns" filled with medicines placed under the eaves or beneath the threshold of his house, where he may suspect his enemy to have already deposited his. He fears for his garden. Thieves are always ready for a raid, if they think they will get off scatheless. So he hangs his horns of medicine on poles at intervals round his plot. He knows that these will protect him and be respected more than all the spring guns or man-traps with which the white man might furnish him for his protection in like circumstances.

To protect his own person, he hangs round his neck a small pad of ash with which his "medical attendant" has provided him as a prophylactic. He trusts in its protective power, for there is a spirit in it, a mystic essence that is more powerful than all the forces that the evil spirits will be able to bring against him for his destruction. His family he will protect in the same way—down even to the baby in arms who wears round its little ankle the tiny rootlet that will afford all the mystic essence needful for its safety and health. All such charms and amulets are supplied by the medicine man "for a fee."

It is in the sphere of disease and death that the Bantu Native finds himself floundering amid the lowest depths of dread of the unseen. The root of all disease and the cause of death he believes to lie, not in the physical destruction of the organs of the body, nor even in their injury or decay. Disease and death are the result of spirit or mystic influences—the work of invisible and intangible agencies. Even accidents resulting in death, a sequence that seems to us unmistakeable, are by him ascribed to the same agency. The sick man, weighed down by this belief, becomes himself an agent in his own illness. Believing himself to be thus beset by powers which are beyond all human aid, he frequently gives way altogether to this mental obsession and loses all desire to live. Thus heartless and hopeless, he precipitates his own end. In such cases, the most common obsession is that the patient believes himself to be bewitched—and against this belief no medical skill in the world seems to prevail. He realises his own parlous state, and ascribes it to the only one possible source. His friends do the same, and between them, the patient slips out of life.

Medical treatment and medicine, therefore, to be effective, he believes, must act on the disease through the spirit that causes it, and so must possess the special mystical property that will meet the case. Mary Kingsley, in her *West African Studies*, says, regarding this subject as she studied it among the negroes of the West Coast of Africa, " everything works by spirit upon spirit ; therefore the spirit of the medicine works upon the spirit of the disease. Certain diseases are controllable by certain spirits in certain herbs ; other diseases are caused by spirits not amenable to herb-dwelling spirits. They must be tackled by spirits of a more powerful grade." [1]

Believing that his own medicine man knows more about these mystic and spirit influences,

[1] See *West African Studies*, by Mary Kingsley, p. 153.

and the medicines that will be effective against them, the Native at first, in all cases, will prefer the treatment of his own Native medical practitioner, to that of the European doctor, however well qualified and skilled he may be. Persuaded against his own better judgment to enter a hospital ward, and after submitting to treatment of, to him, a weird and un-understandable nature, many a time he will appeal to doctor or nurse, saying with tears in his eyes, "Let me go home and drink my own native medicine, and when I am better I will come back to hospital." He may get leave. If he does not, he will run away in the night, and gets home. There he gets better. He is among things and actions and people familiar to him. In the hospital he was a stranger, both to people and treatment. His clothes were taken from him, and mayhap with them some pet charm he was till then never separated from. He was washed and scrubbed, bathed, and possibly treated with applications whose mystical powers may be dangerous to his constitution, and to which he has no antidote. He is laid on a bed, far away from the ward fire—and, greatest deprivation of all, his friends have the little tit-bits of food they were bringing him taken from him. It is not merely the surgeon's knife he dreads—he dreads that too, and most of all, lest some part of what the knife removes may be used as means of secret agency against him—but it is the medical nostrums he is dosed with, which have all doubtless their special spirit powers and mystic influences. Hence the reluctance of the Native to enter the White Man's hospital and submit to the White Man's skilled treatment and attention—a reluctance which the White Man usually ascribes to the Native's ignorance and obstinacy, but which really arises out of a dread, to him perfectly natural and well-founded, and more powerful than his anxiety arising out of his diseases. There is not the least doubt that his mental state acts beneficially or otherwise on his state of health—even though his ailment may be one plainly needing surgical treatment. I have known a native patient, suffering from a diseased limb, which the doctor said could be saved only by serious operation, resisting all inducements to submit to the same, and after many warnings as to the consequences of his action, get himself carried home, having said "Good-bye" with a smile to the hospital and its skilled staff. I have known the same patient, in six months' time, walk into the hospital consulting-room to present the doctor with a fowl, which the abashed recipient had to confess he had certainly not earned. So potent is the Bantu African belief in the mystic elements at work both in disease and medicine.

Among such dark shadowy things of life, the Bantu Native passes his days and his nights of fear—the fear aggravated by the darkness. From anywhere or everywhere these mystic agencies of evil may be working their spell upon him. All through his conscious life he moves knowing nothing, seeing nothing certain, but always with a dread of what this person or that person may be planning or plotting against him, or what this new factor in life which he is meeting may mean to him or for him. Is it to be wondered at if he regards everything novel with suspicion, and that to him suspicion is tantamount to proof? Is it to be wondered at if he was in the early day of the opening up of Africa loth to receive strangers? Knowing the Native as we know him now, we can well understand much of the hostility that early travellers and explorers met with in their first entry into the country. Fearing as he did that these strangers might be the agents of fresh unknown mystic influences, one marvels that they were suffered to enter at all and still less to sojourn in the country. No wonder Stanley was yelled at as he glided down the Congo in his canoes, passing countless villages agog with the dread of what it all might mean for them. And we can understand now how it was that Joseph Thomson was able to pass through the Masai country only by pretending to be a " lybon," a medicine man who had a medicine able to cure the plague that was decimating their cattle, but only after he himself had put ten days' travel between himself and the scene of the cure he was about to effect.

Darkest and most dread of all the shadows that hang ever over the native life, among the many fears that beset him, is the fear of witchcraft. It clouds his outlook almost from earliest consciousness, and it is the last article of his old heathen faith which the Christian convert will abjure, to which, even the advanced Christian, in despair, will refer his misfortune. I have known a tiny schoolboy beseech me to leave my study door open at night after he had passed out, that the light from my lamp might light up the path from the manse to his dormitory, that so he might see to run quickly lest the witches catch him before he reached the shelter of his own dormitory door. I have known men, well advanced in the Christian life, when stricken dumb by some sudden personal family bereavement, throw suddenly aside all they have learned in the years of their Christianity and go back to heathen practices forsaken long ago, seeking for fiendish revenge, against the enemy who had brought desolation into his life. So hard does the old faith fight with the new in the souls of these young native Christians The marvel to me has been the victory they have won in the end—marvel, too, that they stand where they stand to-day.

No accusation is more resented even in jest than that of being partner in the abhorrent practice of witchcraft. It is the deadliest of insults—greater than even an attack on the honour of his mother. The very hint of such an accusation will make the insulted one demand to drink the ordeal poison, to clear his name, and not all the protestations and persuasions of his friends will soothe his sense of damaged honour. Not unfrequently a Native, labouring under such an insult, has gone to the wood to search for the bark of the ordeal tree, and chewed it, in defiant protestation to prove his innocence. Among the Angoni tribe, a whole village, under a charge of witchcraft brought against them by their chief, have drunk the poison together with many fatal results.

The native dread of evil wrought by the witches' spell is equalled by their horror of the ghoulish feasts which the witches make on human flesh, and for the sake of which they carry on their abhorrent practices. Even the innocent tins of preserved meats, brought out by the white man in the early days of settlement to be used in times of local scarcity, have been looked upon with suspicion. I have known a school of fifty young boys and girls emptied of its pupils in two minutes by the mere whisper that their white teacher was that morning building a large brick oven—for which their nervous minds thought there was only one possible use.

Witchcraft is the final, as well as the actual, cause of almost all the misfortunes that enter into the African's life. He knows nothing of the working of the forces of Nature, nothing of the origin, or cause, or nature of disease. In all his vocabulary there is no word for chance —because in his solution of the riddle of life there is no room for chance. He sees some mishap or evil fortune befall him as a "bolt from the blue." Whence was it cast, and by whom? A hundred men and women pass along the path that goes past his house and bends off to the village well—as they have done for years and years. One day his little daughter goes off along that path to the well with a pitcher on her head. This she has done every day since she learned to balance the vessel without grasping it with both hands. But this day as she hurries towards the water a tree falls on her and she is killed. Her father knows nothing of the long process of decay that was eating out the heart of the tree, nor of the white ants devouring its dead roots. He did not take any notice of the strong blast of wind that preceded the rain shower, whose force completed the destruction that decay and the white ant had begun. He could think only of his little child, done to death by its falling boughs, and his whole outlook on life bade him cry out, "An enemy hath done this." Some ill-wisher has by his spells wrought on the child, causing her to pass that way at that fatal moment, or on the tree roots, or the wind-blast blowing over the tree-tops at the same instant. Death has been the result, "An enemy had done it." Somewhere about his hut, under the eaves, or among the thatch of the roof, there are secreted the horns that contain the fatal medicine which a witch has placed there, and which hath brought down this calamity on his household and home.

The whole family life—the whole village life—comes to a standstill. Relatives and near friends gather with the neighbours to mourn at the stricken home. None dare be absent from any cause whatever, lest the suspicion of witchcraft be breathed in association with their name. Relatives are summoned from far and near, and till certain of the more important of these arrive, the burial rites cannot be put through. The women gather in the hut, where the dead is already wrapped up for burial—in the child's ordinary sleeping mat and garments. The men sit in silence outside—and the African knows how to keep silence—even a great multitude of them. As each successive band of mourners arrive, the women join in the mourners' wail for the dead—and their wail is caught up by those inside the hut. African womanhood thus voices its sorrow for the loss of those to whom their pain gave birth; the men brave out their sorrows voiceless. This in the daytime. In the night, the women sleep in the hut beside the dead, the men keep watch with noise of drum and dance, for if they slept the witches who compassed the little girl's death and who wait for an opportunity to reach the corpse that they may make a ghoulish feast of its flesh, might, while men slept, gain their end.

The morrow sees the cortege on its way to the burying place—the appointed bearers carrying the corpse, the rest of the men behind. Behind these again follow the women, clad in their oldest and dirtiest garments—in bark cloth many of them, for death throws man back on his old habits and customs that civilisation is rapidly wiping out. The body is laid on the ground—a sacred spot thenceforward, at which some day offerings will be laid for the spirit of the dead child. The grave is dug—one side hollowed out cave-like, with the opening to the east. There the body is laid—on its side—also facing the east. Then the personal belongings of the child are laid beside it, clothes, blankets, toys—all the things she used while in life. The school-book is torn up and cast in, the slate is broken and laid with it. For the heathen parents had sent the child to school, that she might enter on the new life for which they felt themselves too old. Then the mother is led forward to the edge of the grave, and turned with her back to it, that she may with her feet scrape some of the earth into the grave beside her child. The grave is filled in—the earth beaten hard over the ground, and the whole covered with stones. The hyenas will be prowling round the grave at night—and the witches, too, may pay a visit—unless fear of the *aseketera,* the witch hunters, deters them. Death rouses many passions and fears—but opens no door to hope or comfort in the heathen's soul.

Silent now, the mourners go down to the nearest stream, and bathe, and then return to the village. Again, too, the night is filled with the sound of drum, and song, and dance—that the witches may know the village is awake and may thereby be kept from a visit to the new-made grave.

A few days pass, and the grass hut where the dead slept is pulled down. The first stage in the mourning is past. Now comes the second. "An enemy hath done this." And that enemy must be found, that he or she may be done to death for the deed done, and the land freed from the menace of the presence of one who can use such dreadful spells.

Several steps were open to the mourners. The most usual was an appeal to the diviner—the man of the "lots"—who is consulted on all matters grave or trivial. He throws his "bones" and reads their verdict. Some one is named—generally some old man or woman without friends to speak for them, or some one in place of power or influence who has raised up enemies against himself, and at whose destruction many will rejoice. The diviner knows all the gossip and tittle-tattle of the village, and knows whom to name, and the verdict will be popular. For the old and friendless none dare speak a word, and even for the powerful and influential lips are closed, lest they, by this act, may bring suspicion on themselves, and come under the same condemnation as partners in guilt. The diviner's verdict is rarely accepted as final. The accused must clear himself, and so appeal is made to a higher tribunal. This may take the form of a pot of boiling water, into which the accused plunges his arm, or a bar of red-hot iron, which the accused has to take up with his hand and carry for a certain distance. If he is unhurt, he is innocent. If burnt, he is guilty. Among the Nyanja people the appeal is generally to the ordeal poison—administered in the shape of an infusion of the bark of the "mwabvi" tree, and by the effect of the drinking of this poison the proof of innocence or guilt is demonstrated. If the accused dies, his guilt is proved, and his relatives are called on to pay compensation to the relatives whom his crime has bereaved. "An eye for an eye, a tooth for a tooth"; a life or its equivalent in goods or ivory or other articles of value for the life of the deceased—and the matter is ended. If he recovers, the relatives are called on to pay him compensation for the "moral and intellectual damage," as the law books say—again in the value of a life or its equivalent. And again an appeal will be made to the lots, and the ordeal, till some one is discovered and done to death as the guilty one.

For the lots, or the water, or fire ordeal, there may be substituted the arts of the witch-finder, the *mabisaliro* (the "discloser of secrets")—generally a woman, and she from the Lomwe tribe, who live east of Shirwa—and who are famed for their knowledge of all things connected with the black arts. The *mabisaliro* is credited with the power of "smelling out" the hands of the guilty ones. She comes and lives for some days in the village of the deceased. She listens to the gossip of the village, chiefly of the women as they gather on an afternoon at the pounding place, and discuss the character and reputation of all and sundry in the village. She thus learns who is popular and who is not, who would not, therefore, be missed if removed from the political or social life of the village. At night she prowls among the huts, the villagers cowering within doors. Woe be to him that is seen outside his hut, for when the day for the verdict comes, most likely it will be his name that will be named as the guilty one! For what purpose would he be wandering in the village at night, unless that he might secret or bury the horns with the medicine that is meant for harm. On the final day of her stay, when the verdict is to be given, the witch-finder gathers the villagers into the village courtyard, where she dances herself into a frenzy, which ends in her shouting out the name of the guilty, or smelling the hands of the bystanders and denouncing the culprit in the face of the crowd. Then, spear in one hand and a gourd of water in the other, she makes a procession through the village, followed by a crowd of interested spectators, who watch her every movement. She pours out a little of the water over a suspected spot, and then with her spear digs out the offending "medicine" that has wrought the harm. The offending articles are gathered in a heap on the ground —none daring to touch or remove them till the finder herself, having completed her task, gathers up her spoils and moves away homeward—not without her fee—which may amount to a goat or sheep, or even a slave—according to the fame and status of the woman witch-finder. But the village is purged of witch-craft ; and the inhabitants count the cost small for the relief furnished by her professional services. The accused may appeal against her decision to the ordeal poison, and may thus escape with his life. But rarely, for both diviner and dancer usually measure with fair accuracy the feeling of the village, and a verdict that will be popular will be given by both. The poison mixer knows how to dilute his poison so as to make it produce the desired effect that will prove innocence or guilt.

I once sought and found myself face to face with one of these *mabisaliro*, in a village near Blantyre. She was dancing in the village courtyard, and here and there stopping to dig up some of the secreted spells. When I arrived, she had a heap of them lying on the ground. To the horror of the onlookers I picked them up, took them home with me, and examined them at my leisure—a piece of a tortoise shell, declared from a distance to be a piece of a human skull, the remains of a witches' feast ; a piece of worsted stocking, declared in the same way to be a patch of human hair ; small bones of game, said to be of human origin; and several small horns filled with medicines.[1]

In this case the headman was the accused party. He demanded and drank the ordeal poison, and recovered. Thus the *mabisaliro* and the poison ordeal contradicted each other. This anomaly was explained by the fact that the headman, being possessed of more powerful medicine of his own, was able by its means to counteract the effect of the poison, and thus prove his innocence.

Among the Yaos of Zomba the accused was not even allowed the appeal to the ordeal poison, but, on being named by the diviner, was bound and carried off, to be shut up in a grass hut in the bush to await his execution by fire.[2]

And thus another member of an African tribe was done to death. In old Africa no man

[1] It was not difficult to see that the soil which the witch-finder turned up when she dug out the "spells," had only recently been disturbed and filled in again. To account for its being so easily dug up, she first poured water over the spot. The articles I picked up I took home to my study—while they were there no one was bold enough to enter.

[2] In both cases—the execution by fire and the trial by poison—the occasion was made a public spectacle, and crowds gathered to witness the result. In the latter case, the spectators watched the effect of the poison till they saw it was to have a fatal effect. Then they would rush upon the accused and beat or stone him till he died. His body was cast out into the forest unburied.

or woman died alone—a second was doomed to death as guilty of the death of the first. Mary Kingsley's words regarding West Africa are equally true of the Bantu of East and Central Africa, "The belief in witchcraft is the cause of more deaths in Africa than anything else. It has killed and still kills more men and women than the slave trade. Its only rival is the smallpox." And, she adds, "The terror in which witchcraft is held is interesting in spite of its horror. I have seen mild and gentle men and women turned by it in a moment into incarnate fiends, ready to rend and destroy those who, a second before, were nearest and dearest to them." [1]

The African himself feels the burden and curse brought on him by the practices of those whom he firmly believes to be the cause of death and disaster. Alongside and in hostility to the bands of those who deal in the spells of witchcraft, there has risen up a class of witch-destroyers whose task is to spy out and attack the ghouls at their feasts on the dead whom, by their spells, they have destroyed. They employ two weapons, the hammer and the cord, and hence are named the "hammerers," and the "throttlers." The Native rarely speaks

[1] *Travels in West Africa*, p. 463.

of these classes or orders of witch-destroyers, probably shrinking from such mention as we avoid thinking of the hangman with his rope and scaffold.

Under British rule in Nyasaland, the accusation of witchcraft, as well as the preparation and the drinking of the ordeal poison, are each regarded as a crime of equal gravity. Attempts are consequently made, not infrequently, to evade the law by the administration of the poison to an animal—generally a dog or a fowl. The result of such a test is looked upon as of equal value to that obtained by the administration of the ordeal poison to the accused person himself.[1]

There is no doubt that in many such practices, both of witchcraft and also in its detection, there enters in a great deal of both deceit and self-deception. The terror of the Native, in the face of the occult powers claimed in such practices, lays him open to being deceived. I have alluded already to the "spells" unearthed by the native witch-finder, which consisted largely of faked articles such as the

[1] Under the law as now administered by the British authorities, I have heard whispered complaints that the "country is getting unsafe," owing to the multitude of witches who are now suffered to live instead of being killed off under the old régime.

witches might be expected to make use of in the practice of their craft.

But whether deceiving or being deceived, the Native has unbounded faith in the powers ascribed to both witch and witch-finder. The medicine man has undoubtedly strong belief in his "medicines," and the witch in his "horns." It is impossible to deny that not a few of the "medicines" employed have valuable therapeutical effects—that, no doubt, if investigated, would be of value in the medical pharmacopœia.

When one considers the whole subject of native belief and practice in those occult arts, one is sometimes driven to the feeling, if not the belief, that one is in the presence of malicious and devilish realities that are antagonistic to God and akin to those "principalities and powers, the rulers of the darkness of this world" against which the Apostle confessed himself to be wrestling. One white man who had made his way into the shrine of a "seer" or prophet, who professed to be the mouthpiece or priest of the spirit of an old Mang'anja Chief who lived in a cave among the Mang'anja Mountains, told me that as he approached the shrine where the seer lived, he felt "weighed down by a load of unspeakable things"—a dread and horror that he was in the presence of something unhuman. Science is not to be the utterer of the last word on matters affecting the susceptibilities of the human soul to influences that are not of this earth. Possibly, and here I speak only from suspicion—I have no proof or evidence that I have been able myself to glean either from Natives or from Europeans—the native doctor may make use of some form of hypnotism in his arts. Certainly, the "medicine" called *chitaka*, whatever be its nature, which the Native thief or housebreaker uses, or is said to use to produce profound sleep on the part of those whose effects they are about to plunder, seems to possess something of hypnotic power—so insensible to all that may be going on around and close to him, does it render the sleeper.

While, however, admitting, not willingly, that there is deception in all such practices, where there is so much cheating abroad in every department of his social life, the Native will return again and again to the authority in which he may or may not have lost all confidence, because he has no other explanation of the phenomena of life he sees around him, and no other refuge from the powers that overwhelm him, and because that authority is the only one in his world which professes to explain and deal with its phenomena. He fears the magicians' arts and yet he turns and seeks their aid in the hour of his helplessness and need.

I have dwelt thus long on the native belief in witchcraft, because from that belief falls the darkest of all the shadows that hang over the life of the Native. To him it is the "arrow that flieth by day," for it never fails of its mark. It is, too, the "terror that walketh in darkness," for he knows that night covers the foul fiends at their foul deeds. Drummond's "fellow" that we saw dancing on that Shirwa-Zomba plain, is happy, and care-free, capering under his load, but let him, in the presence of some personal bereavement or calamity, hear the whisper "ufiti" (witchcraft), and the terror of coming evil darkens his eyes, and fills them with a wild gleam of desire for revenge.

I have dwelt thus long on the native belief in witchcraft, because it is also the most powerful factor in his life in determining action or policy. The other elements in his creed, his religious beliefs and practices in relation to the spirit world of which I have spoken, have little or no influence in determining action or duty. His faith in the workings and influences of the witches' powers drive him into action as none other thing does. It is, as I have said, the last stronghold of his heathenism to fall before the Christian faith. Many a time, indeed, long after the soul of the convert has been happy in the consciousness of the great love and care of God in Christ, will some personal calamity bring back the old fear and its wild passion which drive him back into his old savagedom.

This belief in witchcraft lays a strong barrier across the path of native progress, whether of an individual or of a community. Prosperity of one over his fellows is ever looked at with suspicion, as being the result of trafficking with the powers of evil. Jealousy is always rampant in the native mind, and creates enemies that lie in wait, ever ready to strike at the prosperous one. Tokens of special intelligence or skill at once arouse suspicion. Even excessive devotion to the ancestral spirits may be the ground of an accusation of witchcraft. One of the most intelligent natives I have ever met, a young headman rising high among the councillors in the chief court, fled for his life the night the chief died, for he knew that if he waited till the morrow he was a doomed man. His natural abilities had raised up a host of enemies. I have known a native lad, eager for self-advancement, and rapidly earning for himself a position of trust and a fair name for honesty, throw it all up and go home to his village, lest by absence at the time of investigation into the cause of his father's death, he might give ground for suspicion that he was concerned in it.

To dispel this fear, to remove this awful shadow that hangs over every native life and home, and to replace it by confidence in the laws of nature and the working of the loving hand of a beneficient God, is, of all the benefits that the Gospel brings with it, the richest blessing.

LECTURE IV

The Appeal through Native Beliefs

IN the three preceding lectures, I have dealt with the native outlook on life, his conception of the various powers, agencies, and influences at work in it, and his relationship to them. That outlook must always be kept before the mind of the missionary in his efforts to bring the Gospel to bear on the life of the people. For that outlook forms a valuable foundation on which he will be wise to plan the building of the new faith he is seeking to found in the hearts and lives of the people he is endeavouring to reach, and whose mind and lives he seeks to Christianise. The missionary of these new days has abandoned the old attitude to the faiths of the heathen world, which looked upon them as wholly erroneous and must therefore be denounced and set aside. He is taught rather to look for elements of truth among these non-Christian faiths and to utilise them as foundation-stones on which to build up the fabric of truth he has come to teach. As our Blessed Lord used the five small barley loaves and the two little fishes of the Galilean lad to make, with his blessing, a feast for the thousands on the hill slope of Galilee, so will the wise teacher of the Gospel take into his hands the fragments of truth which these native faiths possess, and, with the blessing of the Lord on them, pass them back enriched by the fuller revelation of Divine truth he can throw on them. He will look upon the faiths of such primitive peoples as the gropings of the unaided mind after that light which lighteneth every man, and which our Blessed Lord came to reveal in all its fulness in the Gospel of our Salvation. He will believe that all the truth that is in heathenism is to be found in Christianity, and that all the goodness that is in heathenism is to be found in its completeness in the religion of Jesus Christ. A Gospel, that is to be indeed a Gospel to the heathen, must be the response to his cry after truth and light, and must solve all those problems of life's mystery which he himself had in the past failed to unravel, and satisfy that hunger of the soul which his heathen faith is utterly unable to meet.

Looking therefore at those elements of the

native mind and thought, which in these past three lectures I have tried to educe, our task now is to see how the Christian Gospel responds to the search after truth which those elements have revealed, and how it discloses to the Native the realities of those truths after which his primitive faith shows him to be groping.

To be to the African a Gospel indeed, it must interpret to him that mystical conception of the world, which is the real foundation-stone of his creed, and which colours his whole outlook on life. We have seen that he looks on the whole of the phenomena of the world and of human life, as under the dominion and power of spirit. There is spirit in everything, and spirit is the vital force in every event that happens. He can never get away from the fact that he is surrounded by spirit always and everywhere. We have seen him feel the presence of it, as he hears the crackling of a twig in the forest, as he passes on his way through it and believes that some spirit presence is getting thus into touch with him, so that he must needs respond to it by throwing an answering twig in the direction whence the sound came. We have seen his belief in that spirit presence and possession, in his profound faith in the charm he wears on his wrist and the medicine he rubs into his body, and whose power for good comes from the unseen mystic power that is in it.

Where we have the place and property and influence of spirit—that mystic essence of the universe—so fully recognised as the basic element in every phenomenon of life, we have there a soil already prepared to receive the seed of a Gospel which is above all things spiritual. We have no need, therefore, to prove to the African the existence of the supernatural forces and energies in human life. The belief in these things is there already, and the missionary's task is to show that the highest of all such mystic powers and activities are to be found in the truths which the Gospel of Jesus Christ reveals to the mind and consciousness of men.

May I venture to add this ? In these modern days, when science is probing deeper and deeper into the mysteries that lie beneath the roots of life and life's powers, and is there finding that the ultimate and final cause of things is not matter but something more akin to that which we call spirit, is he not verging on what the African Native, out of the deep need of his own conscious life, has wrought out for himself that, not matter but spirit is the origin and cause of all the phenomena of life; and proving, what the African has made the basis of his religious faith and feeling, that matter and spirit in their mutual influence the one on the other, may lie not so far separate from each other after all. Things that are hid from the wise and prudent are sometimes revealed to babes.

Believing then, as the Native does in the power of spirit over matter, the Gospel story of our Lord's life and work in the world, wherein is exhibited in its most sublime form the power of the spiritual over material things, presents to the Native no difficulty at all. The miracle wrought by our Lord at the pool of Siloam—the anointing of the blind eyes with clay made with the spittle of our Lord—is altogether in the native way of thinking, when he sees his own physicians use the same or similar means in effecting cures of diseases presented to them. Neither does the native convert feel difficulty in the doctrine of the Holy Communion, which teaches that in the Sacrament, the devout communicant is, "not after a corporal or carnal manner, but by faith, made partaker of His Body and Blood, to our spiritual nourishment and growth in grace."[1]

[1] Professor H. A. A. Kennedy's words, quoted by the Rev. Dr. H. J. Wotherspoon in a previous Course of Croall Lectures

It is, however, when we come to the region of spirit and the spiritual in human life that we find how full the response of the Gospel is to the natives' craving after communion with the unseen.

A deeply rooted faith in the existence of a spirit in man is already there. Whether we designate that spirit by the word " spirit " or " soul," or whether we recognise in the human being the existence of both in the tripartite man, as St. Paul does, is not a matter that need give us concern. Few people anywhere seek to differentiate between " soul " and " spirit." What is the relation between the " spirit " that is in man, and what that mystic essence we have called spirit which is in material things, and which Edwin Smith calls " dynamism," or whether there is any relation at all, need not also give us concern. It is enough that our Native believes, that in him there is a spirit that is not material, that does not die with the body, and that has its own continued individual existence in a life beyond the grave.

on the *Religious Value of the Sacraments* bear quotation here. " Sacramentalism is no excrescence of primitive superstition, but corresponds to a permanent demand of human consciousness, the demand that the visible and tangible should be a seal to faith in that which is unseen and eternal."

This faith, together with its natural corollary of faith in the existence of a spirit world into which these individual souls or spirits are gathered needs therefore no proving by the preacher of our Christian Gospel. It is there already, for the Native who never heard the Gospel message in any form, when asked regarding the dead or when reporting, as he does in his own reverent fashion, will say, "He has gone to God."

Whatever significance he may attach to the idea of "God," whether he recognises it as a Supreme Spirit over all other spirit forms, or whether it be to him simply the spirit of some ancient or ancestral chief to which the survivors pay rites of worship, or whether, as I think more likely, it is the term he applies to denote the aggregate of the spirits of the dead in the spirit world, without any attachment of the idea of personality, is not a question either that need concern us. It is enough, I think, for the Gospel to be able to appeal to a great supreme Spirit Power which his hearers at once accept. He accepts, too, without difficulty, the attributes which Christianity discloses to him of a Being in whom dwells the tripartite Fatherhood, the Sonship, and the Spirit emanating forth from the Father and the Son, and revealing both as in the Christian dispensation through Jesus Christ. He will say, " That is new to us," but it lies natural to him in his way of thinking, for the relations of fatherhood and sonship pass within the veil, and subsist there as they did in life.

When we come to that striving after communion between this world and that which lies beyond, which the native faith shows him to be seeking after, the Christian Gospel can meet him with both hands full. The Bridge of Prayer has been built already by the Native craving after this form of intercourse with the spirit world, or with his own dead whom he believes to be still alive there within the unseen. He may appeal to the Spirit of the dead direct, or he may appeal, as some hold, to the Supreme Spirit through the medium of intercession by one who he believes will have influence with that Supreme Spirit. He may seek to make that appeal all the stronger, by offerings such as he would have made to the deceased while on earth. The mighty fact is there, that the African believes, and this belief is universal among the Bantu Race, that God can be approached through prayer, and, the Gospel adds, prayer through Jesus Christ, God's only Son, our Lord. Thus again does the Christian

Gospel fill full the hands that seek to grasp truths that are now to be revealed to him in the great intercession through Jesus Christ our Lord.

In his sacrificial system also, he seeks communion with the dead—communion which he feels death has not broken, for death is to him only the passage out of one state into another—and the veil between is very thin. In this world, soul spoke to soul in the mutual presentation of gifts. A gift given and received was the seal of human fellowship—and in the intercourse between living and dead gifts of sacrifice, in such form as the dead will receive, are still the seals of a friendship that has not been broken.

All this is but the foreshadowing of that great Christian truth which the Scottish Church has almost altogether forgotten, the doctrine of the Communion of Saints. All that the native craves for in his sacrifices and offerings at grave or shrine, that longing for intercourse with the departed who he fondly believes are still alive, the Catholic Gospel can give to the African in its fulness, to add to what he has found for himself.[1]

[1] Our creed says, " I believe in the Communion of Saints," and our Confession declares in interpretation of this faith,

We are thus able now to realise in some small measure how much there is in native belief and thought already cherished by him, to which the Gospel can at once make an appeal. The cardinal truths of belief in spirit, in a spirit world, in a Supreme Spirit in some form or another, in communion with the spirit world through prayer and sacrifice, these the messenger of the Gospel finds ready to his hand—to make the path of the preacher easier to the heart and conscience of the African tribesman.

When I mention "conscience," I remember that I face the strongest barrier that the Gospel has to meet in its presentation and approach to the native mind. In all I have said regarding the spirit and the spirit world, and the relation to it of the human spirit, I have said nothing

that we "share in each other gifts and graces." Out of this fulness of Christian teaching unfortunately, the Scottish Church has retained hardly a fragment, less even than our Native has found in his groping after intercourse with the Unseen. It needed the catastrophe of the War, and the demands of poignant grief for the fallen, to rouse the Church to make what is still but a faltering commemoration, made only, alas, in still but a few Churches, of the Blessed Dead. It is true—alas, that it should have to be said—the Scottish Church has forgotten its dead. A yearly commemoration of the Departed which the festival of All Saints affords would do not a little to keep alive in our hearts a strong faith in the communion of living and dead, which the African is seeking for, and which our Gospel in its fulness richly provides.

of any ethical element in it. And that is because there is no ethical element in it at all. Morality does not enter into the native theosophy, nor in any measure at all into his conception of God or Spirit, or the spirit world, or the future life. The moral state of the living has no bearing on, or relation to, their condition or place in the other world. A cruel, unjust, or wicked chief is appealed to in the spirit world with the same confident approach as to the paragon of all the virtues. There are, as we have seen, good spirits and bad spirits, but these are classed according to their benevolence or malevolence, and not according to any moral quality. Their place and condition in the other world is simply a continuation or renewal of their place and condition in this.

Morality, therefore, gives no place in native character and thought on which we can build any appeal for an acceptance of the Gospel. We find no way of approach through any sense of guilt or consciousness of sin. When any question of moral conduct is present, conscience at no time enters as a deciding factor in native life. The main determining factor in such matters is the fear of consequence which alone deters the Native from any course of moral misconduct, and keeps him in the right path.

I have heard a Native, in a court of law, appeal to fear of the recognised consequences of a moral lapse of which he was accused, as a proof of the unlikelihood of his having committed it. Consequences of the results of transgression, and not any voice of conscience, are the main deterrent factors in native conduct.

In native law there is no such thing as a crime, and therefore, there is no such thing as a criminal code of laws. Every "crime," damage to person or property, is a "tort," and every "criminal action" is really a "civil action" to secure damages. Consequently, every "crime" in native law may be atoned for by payment of compensation according to a certain scale, which generally follows the law of the *lex talionis*, "an eye for an eye," and "a tooth for a tooth"—only the eye, given in payment, is represented by so much native currency, cloth, beads, etc. The "criminal," once he has "tholed his assize," and paid the compensation demanded of him, takes his place again in society, "The case is finished." Any disfavour shown to the criminal for his conduct would arise only from fear of a repetition of the crime, not from any abhorrence of it.

This lack of a sense of crime and the punishment of it as an offence against society or the State, has rendered the institution of British Law, in the British Protectorate, a matter of no small difficulty in the magisterial courts dealing with native cases. The punishment of crime under the new law brings no compensation to the injured party such as he would receive under the old native law. The injured party has, therefore, some difficulty in understanding why none of the fine imposed is paid over to him, in compensation for the damage received. A wiser policy, and one beginning to be followed now in certain cases, is to follow native law instead of British practice, in cases where its imposition would not be contrary to morality and justice.

With such views ruling in the old native courts of jurisdiction, it is not surprising that we can find no conception of sin as a moral lapse or failure. Sin is just a crime to be compensated by payment. In the native tongue there is, therefore, no word for "sin," and none corresponding to our idea of conscience. In the translation of the Bible into the Nyanja tongue, the *lingua franca* of a large part of Central Africa, the translators had to build up a term for "conscience," in which the primary idea was that of "digging," or "rousing memory" in the heart.[1] In the latter case, the word "heart" is used to express the idea most akin in the native mind to that of moral conscience. But this word has such a variety of application that to employ it in the strict sense of "conscience" would often be entirely misleading.

Gradually this word has been Christianised, and is now understood in its new application as standing for "conscience." In the same way, "evil" in the native mind signifies something that is "hurtful" and "damaging"—"ugly," "distasteful," or "displeasing." There is no ethical significance in the word. Murder is "bad," because it is injurious to human life, which may always be appraised at a value. Murder, like other "crime," may be compensated by money payments. Breaches of the moral law, as "lying," "stealing," or even "adultery," are recognised as "evil," only because damaging to property. As in the case of "conscience," the translators of Scripture had to take a word in the native tongue, it may be with sinister associations, and baptise it into Christian usage. For the expression of the idea of "sin," they took a

[1] In Chi-Nyanja, *chikumbu-mtima*, literally "heart-digging," from the two words *ku-kumba*, to dig, and *mtima*, the heart.

8

term which meant only to "err," or to "make a mistake" and adapted it to ethical usage. So that the schoolboy confessing that he had failed to "do" the sum on his slate correctly, used the same word, in the same identical form, as the sinner pouring out his soul in confession before God, "I have sinned." Only in the latter case the word has taken on an ethical meaning, and been baptised into the vocabulary of prayer and devotion.[1]

In times of religious awakening, native converts have not unfrequently been thrown into a state of violent excitement and self-condemnation which evidence all the symptoms of an awakening or awakened conscience. Scenes such as in Christian countries have been witnessed in connection with times of religious revival of a pronounced evangelical type, have occurred among the native community. In some cases I have experienced, following on the appeals of an earnest evangelical type, it was only the presence and control of the presiding

[1] The nearest approach to anything like the expression of a sense of guilt is that which, in native life, is known as *chilope*, or "murdergeist." It is supposed that the spirit of a slain man haunts the murderer. To obviate this the Angoni-Zulu warriors disemboweled the dead slain in battle, a practice which is believed to prevent such an eventuality. In this case, however, the consequences are purely physical, and can in no way be looked upon as the result of movings of conscience.

minister or interpreter that kept the members of the congregation from bursting into violent excitement, and self-accusation of sins real or imagined.[1]

Keeping in view what I have said as to the difficulty if not the impossibility of an appeal to conscience, so as to evoke a sense of sinfulness, to what then is the Gospel to appeal in the first instance, and what form is the appeal to take ?

In a former lecture, I alluded to the African

[1] In his book on *Winning a Primitive People*, the Very Rev. Dr. Donald Fraser describes such scenes in a revival that took place at his mission station in Central Africa. " The intensity of feeling required to be carefully guided, lest physical emotions be mistaken for true religion, and fervour waste itself in harmful or futile directions. One morning two of the leading teachers came to me to relate strange experiences they were having. They had been out in the bush at night praying. They felt as if their bodies had been lifted up from the earth, and bright angelic forms had come to meet them. They asked me to explain what these visits meant. Instead of doing this, I went through to the dispensary, and getting two big doses of salts, gave each of them a dose, and sent them off to bed."

A fellow missionary of Dr. Fraser's told me that he found the same treatment effectual in the case of some enquirers who came to him labouring under the heavy burden of a troubled conscience, which evidenced itself in self-condemnation of grievous sin, but which he diagnosed as the working of physical excitement. Yet out of such occurrences as these, Dr. Fraser bears testimony to the " strong piety which burst into bloom at that convention, and which remains with them still in increasing beauty."

"instinct" for character—and his appreciation of the place and value of character in personal influence. This instinct enables him to form a wonderfully accurate estimate of persons with whom duty or business brings him in contact. This is particularly evident in his estimate of the characters of the white man whom he deals with as Master or Teacher. I have seen instances of an intuitive knowledge of character that seemed almost uncanny. It is character alone that will secure for the white man respect —and true influence. He may command obedience from his official position, or his material resources, or from any worldly advantages which he may have it in his power to confer; but character and character alone, win him that loyal and affectionate service which the African is capable of rendering in rich measure to both master and teacher.

It is through this instinct for character and his appreciation of the higher qualities of life, with which character is associated, that the Gospel finds its readiest appeal to the heart of the Native; and, through appreciation of the highest source of that character, he is drawn to the Christian faith. The youngest Christian, born anew, imperfect though he often is, wins his admiration and then his envy. "What was it that first led you to think of Christ and Christianity?" I have asked my young candidates for entrance into the catechumenate. I have had various answers. "It was a dream," some said. "It was the reading of the Word of God," said others. "It was a sermon"—this not very frequently. Most frequent of all was the answer, "It was Thomas—or James—or Luke," naming some Christian convert or companion whose changed manner of life had stamped itself on his admiration. This impact of the Christian character on the mind and conscience of the African, is, I believe, the greatest power the Gospel wields in bringing him to a knowledge of himself, and his moral and spiritual needs. Under the power of the grace of God it is the means of evoking the voice of conscience, hitherto dormant, but waiting the call of Christ to awake to life.

When, however, to the appeal of character as evidenced in the fruits of Christianity, which, imperfect though they be, are far in advance of the best fruits of heathenism, we add the appeal from the character of our Blessed Lord Himself as portrayed for us in the Gospel story, we feel we have found the heart of the Gospel message to the soul of the African. The

Gospels, rather than the Epistles, form the primer of the Christian life from which the convert gets his highest teaching as to what Christianity is and what it demands of him. The Gospel reveals the new religion as a life and a character which the African can understand. Our Lord's declaration of the end and object of His mission into the world meets in every letter of it the need of the African, and commands his approval. "I am come that they might have life, and that they might have it more abundantly." The Saviour that will draw and retain the homage of the African, is a Saviour unto life—a Saviour that will lead him into a life and character like His own. He—the African—must recognise the attraction of Christ before he can come to a consciousness of his own sinfulness. He must come face to face with the Holiness of the Saviour, before he can realise that sin of his own from which the Saviour Christ alone can save him. The sense of sinfulness in the African is a product of his Christian faith, not the origin or cause of it.[1]

It comes to the convert as an after-fruit of his

[1] In his book, *The Living Forces of the Gospel,* Warneck says: "In the case of most Christian converts from heathenism, it is not the knowledge of sin that leads to Christ the reconciler; it is Christ the Redeemer who leads to a knowledge of sin."

touch with the living Christ as he sees His image in His converts, and as he sees Him as He is in Himself clearly and perfectly in His portraits drawn for us by the writers of the Gospel History. Drawn by the Spirit of God to the original of that portrait, the Living Christ, he finds himself in the presence of a perfect character; and a new moral outlook opens before him. He sees sin now no more as a thing redeemable by a price, nor as a mere mistake causing injury or damage, but as something that comes between himself and the perfect ideal he sees before him in the Christ. He sees sin as a barrier between himself and the Holiness of God evinced in Christ, as a blot on that perfect character of Christ which he is called on to strive after. He views now his relation to God from a moral point of view, and religion, instead of being a thing of sacrifices and offerings, and amulets and taboos, becomes a moral influence in his life, making moral claims on him, and promising moral rewards. New forces enter into his soul's life that come from what God is, and what man is. The Gospel, with its portrait of the Man Jesus Christ, creates a hatred of sin and a craving after that holiness whose character is seen in Christ, and the convert learns through contemplation of that perfect life of holiness, that only by a life of holiness a continuous communion with God becomes possible.

Old heathen rites and customs are now viewed in a new light, and made to pass through the crucible of a newly awakened conscience, and by it are tested in the light of the new conception of holiness. The meaning of much that has hitherto been accepted as the traditional customs received from his ancestors, is examined afresh in this new light, and henceforth conscience becomes a leading factor in habit and custom, instead of the old heathen traditions.

This new-born sense of sin begets the thought of atonement or ransom—a thought that is never far from a native's mind in connection with his idea of crime, even as a civil misdemeanour. In the native conception of sacrifice, in connection with his religious ceremonial, there is no idea of the offering taking the place of either the offerer or anything else. Sacrifice in the native ritual is either a mode of propitiation or a means of expressing thankfulness. These gifts are in no way substitutionary—they are simple gifts offered in an effort to please and perhaps obtain some benefit from the Being to whom the worship in this form is paid.

Notwithstanding this lack of substitutional ideas in sacrifice, the idea of substitution itself is engrained deep in native thought. Ransom is a recognised means of freeing one—oneself or another—from an obligation or penalty. Atonement by literal substitution as we have seen is common practice in native life, " an eye for an eye," " a life for a life," " a slave for a slave," or its equivalent value. Such ransom covers all the fault, and the wrong is atoned for ever.

In the case of a chief or headman, his responsibilities are greater than those of an ordinary individual, and extend to a wider area. He is responsible not for himself alone, but for every one of his subjects. What they do he is liable for, and what he does for them, is their doing. The chief or headman takes the misdemeanour, or fault, or crime of his people or villagers on himself, and the ransom paid by him for them is accepted as if paid by themselves, and thus the chief's ransom closes the case.

It is not a long way from this to the Christian conception of Atonement, in which that Atonement, made by Christ as the Head of the Human

Race, is accepted as made by his people because of their union with Him in the mystic body of His Church. The convert looks on the Cross, and sees on it the Head of humanity laying down His life for the sin of men—making their atonement or ransom for them—he sees himself, by virtue of his union with Christ Himself, sharing in the benefits of that ransom, just as the subjects of the old native chief shared in the benefits of the ransom paid by him. "He bare our sins in His own body on the tree," "I was crucified with Christ," are truths of our faith that therefore present no difficulty to our convert's way of thinking. They are in the line of his thoughts already as he considers the relationship that exists between him and his chief, and this renders the thought of the atonement for sin made on the Cross a natural and easy one for him to accept.

When we come to the domain of fear which we have seen cast so deep a shadow over all native life, we realise how much the Gospel message means to him, in lifting the clouds of superstition which cause that fear, and deepen its every shadow. We realise how real is the sense of freedom which the Gospel brings to a mind emerging from a region of darkness into the clear light of the realities of things.

The fear of offended spirits, the fear of the spells and charms of his earthly enemies plotting destruction, and above all, the awful dread of the demoniacal powers of witchcraft—the freedom from these things I can compare with nothing else African than that marvellous story of Stanley's march for months through the gloom of the Congo Forest, on to the clear sunny treeless plains that lay in front of them all the way to the Albert Lake. The wild ecstasy of joy which his followers exhibited when, instead of the gloom of the sunless forest, they saw overhead the bright sun and the blue sky, is but a type of the joyousness that comes to the African's soul, when the light of Christianity dawns on it. To see a patient in a hospital ward, lying day by day, dull, listless, speechless, without any attempt to bestir himself, without any desire to live, is to know but faintly, and that from the outside, what must be the fears that enshroud the soul of a man who believes he is the victim of a witch's spells. To cast into that man's soul a light that shows him the great love of God, to teach him that disease and suffering and death are not the work of witchcraft but the laws of Nature which are the laws of the God whose name above all else is Love, is to bring to him a

Gospel indeed. The little school lad of whom I spoke in a previous lecture, begging me to let my study door remain open for a little that the light might show him the path by which he could run swiftly to his dormitory and evade the powers of darkness lying in wait for him, is a parable of all heathen Africa seeking a light which the Gospel alone can afford in its brightness.

While we remember all these things, we, on the other hand, do not forget that this fear of what might follow the neglect of duty to the dead, or the breach of some tribal or family rule of life, or the wilful breaking of a taboo for the sake of indulgence in unlawful lusts, has undoubtedly done much to keep native society free from moral lapses that would lead to the destruction of all the moral laws that bind society and family life.

All the more reason, therefore, that in these days when the tide of civilisation flowing so rapidly all over Africa threatens even native morality at its very foundations, we should replace the old form of superstitious restraint by the power of self-control that comes from the grace of God. What Chalmers called "the expulsive power of a new affection," can come in its highest and best form from that fear and love of God which casteth out all other fear, and gives the soul, rescued from darkness, a place in the Kingdom of God, "which is righteousness and peace and joy in the Holy Ghost."

LECTURE V

How the Seed is best sown

IN the course of the past four lectures we have been studying the Native of Central Africa in his ordinary daily environment as most strangers see him, but we have also endeavoured to penetrate some little distance into that inner mind of his which is still an enigma to the white man, and which will ever be an unknown region to the white man until the Native himself turns his mind inward on himself and tells us what he finds there. Till this is done we enter on the consideration of the most fitting appeal that the Gospel can make to him with the feeling that our efforts are but tentative. Remembering, therefore, this limitation of our subject, I come now to the practical question of the best methods of bringing our Christian faith into touch with the heart and mind of these Native peoples. We have seen that the Gospel of Christ—if it is to be a gospel to the African at all—must be a gospel of life

—coming to him and meeting him in his life to-day as our Blessed Lord came to the world—voicing his mission in his own pregnant words, "I am come that they might have life, and that they might have it more abundantly." To bring to the African this abundant life is the task which the messenger of the Gospel has to discharge. How is he to enter on this task? What means is he to use to bring this new life to the African as we find ourselves face to face with him in his daily life?

It is a question that in the early days of pioneer mission work the missionary had often to ask himself, "How am I to begin?" He found himself settled among a new people—alone, possibly miles and miles from any other Christian soul—no one with whom he could exchange a word of sympathetic fellowship or to whom he could unburden a soul on which his new task lay heavy. Around him was a native community—maybe a whole tribe, of whose tongue he had learned only a smattering—if anything at all. Of their manners, habits, and customs he knew nothing—nothing of their psychological outlook on life which was to be, even after many years, still a sealed book to him. Those stolid yet wondering faces, which jostled each other round his tent or grass shed that meantime housed him and his belongings, their eyes watching every movement and gesture—they were all alike to him. They crowded about him—making their presence felt to more than one of his senses—the bolder venturing even to handle his few possessions—in some cases with insidious attempts to change their ownership. Most insistent of all, and yet one whose good graces had to be secured at all costs, was the chief or headman himself. He had probably welcomed the presence of the missionary—not from any desire to hear the Gospel, but from a shrewd hope of worldly benefits or improved status to himself among his neighbouring chiefs accruing to him from the presence of the white man in his country. How many a pioneer missionary has been described—naming the chief, as "so-and-so's White Man!"

The young missionary has not long been settled before he realises that the African has no desire for his teaching, nor any sense of the need of that Gospel which the missionary has come to impart. His limited knowledge of the Native tongue keeps him from understanding much of the talk going on daily around him. He sees enough, however, during those few months to make him conscious of the difficulty of the task he has set his face to, and to ask himself, " How am I to begin ? "

The best answer is to seek for no answer—but just to begin—to begin with the task lying immediate to his hand. This, in the experience of every pioneer missionary, is to build his station—to employ and possibly to teach his Native workers their tasks—to work alongside them, to live among them day after day, week after week—all the while watching them and studying them—learning more and more of their language, more and more of their tribal habits and customs—getting daily nearer and nearer to them—though feeling as if they were receding more and more from him, in thought, in feeling, and in mutual understanding one of the other. That on his side. But on their side while he is studying them—they are studying him—with that wonderful instinct of theirs for character, they are reading him through and through. With keen microscopic eyes they mark his little traits of character—any weaknesses he may display are rapidly noted—characteristics he may hardly be aware of himself at all. Every hour of the day he is under observation. And then in the evening round the village fire, or on the flat rock where the women place the mortars in which they pound their household grain, he is discussed, his character for patience or kindliness or courtesy, or that "good heart" which stands so high in Native estimation. These are all weighed and measured with an accuracy that would astonish the subject of it all and make him think more humbly of himself. While, therefore, he is thus learning to know his people, his people are learning to know him.

And that is how he begins. That is his first sermon, his first lesson of religious instruction —the best lesson he will ever teach during all the after years of his work in Africa—the lesson of his own life.

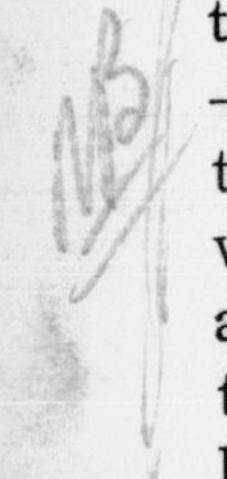

That is how the Gospel must be brought home to the soul of the African—the Gospel of a life —a character—something which the most untutored Native can understand, something which the most advanced Christian will more and more realise as his ideal to reach forward to—though still far away. This Gospel of a life the missionary teaches himself—in school, in class, in workshop, in church, a life of personal Christlikeness.

But there is in addition the lesson taught by the community life of the mission members, preaching the Gospel of a Christian Society, showing by the harmony which runs through the work of the mission community the mutual forbearance one with the other, and the sacrifice of self which inspires the actions and characters of all the mission agents. The African eye is keen to note any lack of unity or any failure of that mutual sympathy and helpfulness which runs through all right community life. The old missionary monks, living as they did under strict rules, were saved from many dangers in this connection that the modern missionary is ofttimes sadly prone to.

Believing, then, that the Gospel has to be presented to the African as a life, the question now arises in what manner and form is that life to be presented to the African so that he may meet and satisfy every part of his nature, both as an individual and as a member of a community. By what means is the Christian life to be brought home to him as the ideal for his own personal life as well as for the life of that society in village and family of which he is a member.

In the presentation to humanity of the life of our Lord as portrayed in the Gospel story, we get a guide to that presentation of the Gospel which will best draw the heart and meet the deepest need of the African people. This portrait of our Lord on earth reveals Him in His home in Nazareth working as a handicraftsman for His daily bread, bearing Himself the curse of Eden which God's mercy changed into humanity's greatest blessing. As the Apocryphal Gospel says, "He made ploughs for the villagers of Galilee." He took on Himself the lot of man to labour, and put His seal on it as part of that abundant life He had come to bring to the human world, and which man was to seek after and claim for himself.

The Gospel to the primitive races of Africa must take into account this element of labour in its presentation of itself as the life more abundant. In his primitive state the native lives on a very narrow plane. His wants are few, and easily satisfied. With only a small amount of trouble he can provide for the wants of himself and those dependent on him. I have already suggested more than one reason why the Native has been so long content with the minimum of the intelligent use of the resources of the land he lives in. To put into his hands, therefore, the power to develop and utilise all these resources, is a step towards attaining that fuller life in which he is now called to share.

In the presentation of the Gospel given by our Central African Missions in Nyasaland at

Blantyre and Livingstonia, we have endeavoured from the first to give this aspect of the Evangel a not unimportant place. As part of our system of missionary training we impart to the more intelligent of our pupils a knowledge of the simpler arts and crafts of civilisation—elements in a fuller and wider type of life than his own. We do this that he may thus be able to make use of his own powers of body and intellect which God has given him, and also that he may use this new knowledge in the development of his country's resources, and making for himself a wider and a stronger environment. This is imperative if he is to meet the new forces and influences which civilisation is now pouring into his country, and threatening in many ways to sweep him off his feet. These new forces will demand his aid in their efforts to introduce new elements into the government, the commerce, the agriculture of this new country, and if he is unable through lack of skill or will to afford that aid, they will turn elsewhere, as in some instances they have already done, with disastrous results to the moral, social, and economic life of the African themselves. Moreover, also, this training of the African in the arts and crafts of civilisation not only gives him the ability to share in the development of his country, but also enables him to build up a civilisation, a social and economic life of his own suited to his own nature and character, and adapted to the changing circumstances of his new life. The conditions of a primitive people call for this education. The older races of the world need no such instruction. They have already built up for themselves in past generations a social life and polity of their own. The Missions in India and China and North Africa have no need to give such industrial, social, or economic training as we have done, and are doing, in Blantyre and Livingstonia. Their own old civilisation is better suited to them than anything that we from the west can give them. Not so the Central African. On the side of thought and culture and skill in arts and crafts he meets the Missionary with empty hands. His hoe, his axe, and his knife, are all he has with which to make a home for himself or carve out a social or economic life of his own. These are not enough in the present developments of the world's enterprise to meet the coming changes in his environment. He must get a wider and firmer grasp of the resources of the world around him. To help him towards this wider and fuller life, I hold to be part of the Missionary's task in the presentation of the Gospel he takes to these races.

Some say this task should be the duty of Government. Yes! but then Government takes up a strange attitude towards religious teaching. Although they profess to believe that the education of these primitive peoples must be founded on "religion and morality," yet as regards the type of religion, Government declares itself to be neutral—a strange attitude for the Government of a nation professedly Christian to assume. That, however, is the situation to-day. Since, therefore, Governments assume the attitude of neutrality in this matter, it is all the more incumbent on the Christian Mission to combine this type of instruction in their work with that more directly religious as part of the Christian Gospel which they are there to teach. An unchristian civilisation in Africa—a civilisation without the grace and power of the Christian faith to control its life and mould its character, would be a disaster beyond measure.

On the other hand, there are not a few supporters of African Missions who hold that the missionary should confine his task to the simple teaching of the Christian faith and the preaching of the Word of God, leaving the Native to continue in his old primitive habits and surroundings such as he lived in before the advent of the new order of civilised enterprise brought him into the open and face to face with the new world at his door. Were this attempted, and where it has been attempted, the African himself would come forward—as indeed he is doing to-day—with a demand for an education which would enable him to meet the new situation and take his place in it. One of the first evidences of a change in an African's heart is an attempt to change his mode of living—better clothing, better housing, better social conditions in his village. The Christian home in an African village is easily noted from its neatness, cleanliness, and an effort—pathetic sometimes in its simplicity—to adapt what he conceives to be the ways of civilised life out of materials he finds ready to his hand. His house will contain substitutes for simple articles of furniture, chairs, a table, a cupboard made of a packing-case, pictures cut from society "illustrateds" on the wall—marks of an effort to raise himself on to a higher plane of home life. But better than all, the husband and wife will sit down together with the family at meals—a revolution indeed in native society, for it means that the wife now takes her place as the equal and the helpmate of her husband, instead of being largely his chattel.[1]

The second element in the life of our Lord's earthly ministry was his ministry of healing. In this, too, the messenger of the Gospel does well to follow the example of our Lord, and carry with him to his task either himself, or through skilled agents, a care for health of the body as a significant part of his mission. The hand of medical doctor and nurse, laid on the diseases and sores of the dwellers in those African huts and villages, fulfils the healing ministry of Christ among the cities and towns of Galilee, and in the temple courts and streets in Jerusalem. They, perhaps, more than any other class of missionary, can preach that practical sympathy of Christianity with the sufferings of humanity which lies so near to the heart of the Christian Gospel. These both doctor and nurse represent to the untaught

[1] I have heard a missionary boast that he had baptized a convert wearing a loin cloth of bark as his sole garment. My own experience of converts to Christianity among the Africans has been that the first token of a changed heart is a new respect for both body and person, shown in neatness and cleanliness of garment. It has been my further experience that carelessness, untidiness, indifference to the outward person are the first signs of deterioration in the moral life and backsliding in the ways of Christian profession. Truly there is in Africa "a philosophy of clothes."

heathen in a manner they can understand the Christ as the Saviour of men's bodies, the healer of the wounds inflicted oftentimes by the indifferences of man to his brother man. No gospel appeal comes nearer to the heart of the suffering helpless heathen, crying, "Make me whole," than the response of the skilled physician "Be thou clean."

Apart from the actual relief of disease and suffering which follows the task of the medical missionary—whether doctor or nurse—there is in addition the lesson daily taught in the dispensaries and wards of our Mission Hospitals of the great brotherhood of all humanity. I have already alluded to the limited idea of mutual responsibility of man for his fellow-man which the native conception of clanship imposes. The African is kind and helpful to his fellow-clansman, for whom he will put himself to endless trouble and on whose behalf he will sacrifice many personal advantages. Within the circle of the clan circumference, sympathy ends. Within the wards of a Mission Hospital the patients see Christian sympathy stretching itself as wide as humanity. Doctors, nurses, and native medical attendants are there seen carrying skill and sympathetic relief from ward to ward in which lie patients of many tribes

and many clans—without distinction one from the other. What the Native attendants see the European doctor and nurse do, they themselves do likewise and with no barrier of clanship to narrow their widened sense of brotherhood. The old plea of callous indifference is gone for ever—" He is not my brother," and in its place the Christian ideal, " All one in Christ."

To the influence of medical mission work in eradicating from the Native mind the fear of witchcraft I have already alluded. When the Native medical student sits at the microscope prying into the secret forces of disease in the form of germs and parasites, there can hardly be room for that most deadly of all superstitions, belief in the power of witchcraft. Like many a product of ignorance it will take wings and disappear before the entrance of knowledge and truth, and, like other native beliefs that cloud the heart and stupify the intellect with fear, this last stronghold of heathen faith will fall before the forces of Christian love and scientific discovery.

The third element in our Lord's earthly ministry—the Gospel of His preaching and teaching—finds its counterpart in the education imparted in the mission schools and native churches. It is part of that " life more abundant " which the Christian faith brings with it. Education means development—the drawing out of the powers and capabilities that have hitherto lain dormant. What these powers and capabilities are in the case of the African has yet to be proved. There are some who would class him mentally very low on the intellectual level. That is no criterion of future capabilities. Dion Cassion measured the inhabitants of the British Isles in his day on a very low scale when he described them as " liars, thieves, and murderers." Pope Gregory, on the other hand, saw a vision of the future in the faces of the blue-eyed, fair-haired boys from Britannia whom he found in the slave market at Rome. " They are called ' Angles ' ? Then they will become ' Angels.' Their king is Aelle ? We will teach them to sing the ' Alleluya.' " The life work and character of such a man as James Aggrey justifies every missionary in looking for great possibilities in the African people.

To meet the needs of the situation of the African peoples, the conception of the Gospel which is to bring the abundant life to him must be founded, therefore, on a wide basis. Christ's ministry was to meet the whole necessities of human life. A Gospel which is to be a Gospel of life must in the same way meet every want in the life of the men and women to whom it is sent. It must reach him not only in his spiritual life, but must satisfy his intellectual life and enter into every department of his family life, his village life, and his community life. The education of the future that will meet the needs of the African people must touch him at all these points. Nothing that ministers to the well-being of these people, body, soul, and spirit, must be considered outside the scope of the Gospel that is to be the saving of his whole life if it is to be to him indeed a Good News. *Nil humanum alienum puto* must be the motto of the African teacher of to-day.

Realising this, the modern mission to Africa is broadening the basis of its educational policy for these primitive people. Government, too, realising its responsibilities for the welfare of the people within its Protectorates, has come to the aid of the educational efforts of the missions in Central Africa and seeks to co-operate. But then Government co-operation may make that extraordinary stipulation that in all matters of religion they must be neutral —which means that Christianity along with other religions is practically ruled out. How can we have an education worthy of the name without Christianity as its controlling and sanctifying power? Government policy would produce a community of educated heathen. The conditions of the African peoples demand that the education of the future produce a community of educated Christians, a community of men and women into whose hands education has put powers far beyond those of their primitive state, but to whom also Christianity gives the grace to control and use those powers.

The banishment of the Gospel from our African schools would be disastrous. Out of the schools in Africa has sprung the Christian Church. The daily Bible lesson in those rude grass-walled, grass-roofed huts that form the village schools of to-day, has revolutionised the whole life of Central Africa—and founded it on a new Christian basis. Out of the school has risen the Church, and it is to the Church and the life and teachings of the Church that the African must look for the interpretation and satisfaction of those mystic longings and aspirations, which are evidenced in the native attitude to the spirit world and which he seeks to satisfy by his search after communion with his dead. The Church must interpret to him the reality of that mystic spirit that he believes to lie in all the phenomena of the natural world in their relation to him and to each other. The Church must interpret to him that belief in the solidarity of clan and family life, that sense of mutual responsibility which has done so much to preserve the community and tribal life from anarchy and self-destruction. This the Gospel —the message of the Church to the human heart—professes to do, and through its life, worship, teaching, and sacraments is doing to-day all over Central Africa.

The conception of the Church as a living body, each member of which has its place and function in which he is responsible for the welfare of his fellow-member, is not a difficult one for one accustomed to think of the unity of clanship or the intimate relations of chief and people. Even the observance of the taboo at the time of some village celebration or festival, the breaking of which would bring misfortune to the whole village community, has had its function in training the native mind to the practice of self-sacrifice and self-denial in the daily facts of human life. All these instances of mutual dependence and mutual responsibilities for each others welfare are fulfilled in St. Paul's teaching, "Ye are members one of another." "If one member suffers, all the members suffer with it." "No man liveth to himself and no man dieth to himself." To these words even the heathen will agree, for they express that mystic unity which he already recognises in clan, family, and village community.

But the conception of the Christian Church will bring him a wider and fuller sense of unity than he has ever hitherto conceived of in his village, clan, and tribal institutions. By his membership in the Church he is brought into a new relationship with peoples and races, with tribes and tongues living far away from the villages on the Shiré Highlands or along the shores of Lake Nyasa. A striking instance of this occurred several years ago under my own observation—an instance of that feeling of unity and mutual responsibility which is one of the pleasing fruits of Christianity. Thirty years ago, on the occasion of a great famine in India, the members of the young Christian Churches in the Blantyre Mission, on hearing of the sufferings of their fellow Christians there, "determined to send relief to their brethren" in the Punjab. I have a vivid memory of the sigh of sympathy which arose from my congregation on the Sunday morning when I described to them the straits into which their fellow Christians in India had fallen. They knew from experience in past years what famine meant, but for the first time in their lives they realised the new bond of brotherhood which Christianity had woven for them with a people in the far-off, hitherto unknown land of India.

The Church, however, that brings to the African the message of the Gospel does not come to him empty handed with nothing to show as the credentials of its mission.

The Church brings the Holy Scripture as the guide of life and the supreme rule of faith and conduct. The Bible in the vernacular tongue is now in the hands of the Nyanja-speaking people of Nyasaland and Rhodesia, and parts of it are also in the hands of other tribes speaking divers tongues into which God's word has been translated. The Bible has had always its right place in all the Mission in that part of Africa, and, as I have already said, from the simple Bible lesson taught by the Native teacher in the village school, the Church of Central Africa has grown. School and Church have hitherto gone hand in hand, a combination and partnership which in the past did so much for the religious life of our own homeland.

But the Church further brings to the Christian

convert the Sacraments of the Christian Gospel. Taking the definition of a Sacrament that given in our Shorter Catechism as a "Holy Ordinance instituted by Christ wherein by sensible signs Christ and the benefits of the new covenant are represented, sealed, and applied to believers," or the definition of a sacrament given in the "Catechism" of the Church of England as "the outward and visible sign of an inward and spiritual grace," and remembering that to the native the virtue of his old charms and the application of them lay not in the material substance of which they were made, but in their inward and mystic essence, it is not difficult, as I have already said, to lead the convert to realise the true doctrine and spiritual value of the sacrament, whose grace and blessing come "not after a corporal or carnal manner" but "by the blessing of Christ and the working of His spirit on them that by faith receive them."

Of the two sacraments, we have in the communion of the Lord's Table the reality of which his communal sacrificial feasts and festivals are but the foreshadowing. By these feasts he believes himself to be brought into communion and fellowship with the spirits of the dead or with that aggregate of the spirit world which, as I have said, stands to him for God. In the Christian sacrament of the Lord's Table a communion is sealed to us, not only with the Lord and Master of the Feast, but with each other, as we together partake of the mystery of "His Body and Blood to our spiritual nourishment and growth in grace." And beside all this there is that doctrine of the communion of saints by which we are partakers of each other's gifts and graces in the life and faith of Jesus Christ our Lord—a "communion" that is not confined to those who are alive but which, accepted in its fulness, will satisfy that longing in the native soul after fellowship with his dead to which the sacrificed worship of his primitive days gives so prominent a place.

The association of the Gospel message with the ordered and orderly rule and government of the Church further commends itself to the Africans' sense of order and fitness. The African is in no way a lawless [1] man, nor is he ever a law unto himself. He is a strict disciple of law and order. From childhood to age he is bound by the customs of his forefathers and of his tribe, and tenders implicit obedience to their demands. He has a precedent or rule or

[1] "A lawless man," Nyanja; *munthu wosaweruzika*; literally an "uncommandable man."

custom for almost every possible situation, social or political, by which he may be faced. The Council of Elders gives the chief sage instruction and guidance, and he is a wise chief who listens and follows. Their loyalty to their chief on the part of his subjects I have already alluded to. Obedience to ordered law and government thus enters largely into the African character, and forms a valuable asset to the organisation of the Church. "What is the law of the Church?" is a question often put by the younger members of Session or Presbytery, and added reverence is given to any practice that has come down from the fathers.

Forgetfulness of this trait in native character has been the cause of no little trouble to both Government and settlers in their relation with the native chiefs and owners of territories. Newcomers fail to realise that the Native has a definite code of rule and precedence in the relation of chiefs and people and the relations of the subjects of the chiefs among and between themselves. Native memory goes far back, and he can give chapter and verse for his claim to any right of which he may think he has been unjustly deprived. Lawless he is not, and never was. The African, with his sense of orderliness and obedience to law, will thus bring a valuable gift into the treasury of the Churches' organised life.

The question of what form such organised life should take is one that no one can or dare attempt to answer at this early stage in the history of the Church in Central Africa. Naturally each mission will set itself to organise its converts on the lines of the system of government which rules in the Mother Church of the mission. A Presbyterian Mission will order its daughter church on the Presbyterian system, an Episcopalian Mission on Episcopalian lines, and so on in the many forms of Christian activity in the homeland. How far these various systems of Church practice will meet the mind of the African when he reaches the stature of full Christian manhood is a question that no one can yet answer.[1]

The young African Church has yet much to learn, especially in the matter of the management of its finances. But assuredly the day

[1] In a meeting of Church leaders recently held at Blantyre, the question was put to them as representatives of over a half dozen different tribes and languages in Central Africa, as to what language would become in time the *lingua franca* of the whole of Central Africa. "We will settle that for ourselves in due course," was the reply. I felt at the time that it was an answer to more than one question as to the future of the race in Central Africa.

will come—sooner perhaps than we at present dream, when the Native Church will ask to be set free to order its own life in its own way. Those missions, therefore, act wisely who guide their daughter Churches on lines that reach back through the past of generations of experience, from which the Church will learn to guide its feet on paths that are well trod. In this connection Pope Gregory's advice to St. Augustine, when he sent him to revive the Christianity of England, should not be forgotten. "Choose," he said, "from among other forms of religious order and experience that which is best suited to the converts you make." Nor perhaps should the maxim of the Latin father be neglected, "*Securus judicat orbis terrarum*,"—he is safe who takes the whole world into view.

This, however, may be said truly regarding this question of the future system of Church government in Central Africa, that the normal form of civil government among these Central African tribes is that of the chief or headman ruling in his council of elders—a system that might be represented in the rule of the Church to-day as that of the Bishop in his Synod of Presbyters and of the Minister in his Session of Elders.

This also must be added, that personality counts for much to the African, and draws out his highest loyalties. He looks to a leader, be he Governor, Bishop, or Minister, and the leader that wins his highest respect will never fail in securing ready obedience.

Our duty to-day in the sphere of missionary enterprise is simple, to give to the African the Gospel with an ordered and orderly Church life and rule behind it, and to leave the future form of government of the Church itself, believing in the continued guidance of the Holy Spirit of our Lord, " Lo, I am with you always, even unto the end of the world."

LECTURE VI

Problems to be faced

THE messenger of the Gospel, entering a country and commencing work among a people untouched by Christianity, has to face questions and solve problems which the preacher or teacher in a Christian country is never called on to deal with. All the more need, therefore, that the pioneer missionary, in addition to the other qualifications essential in such a task, should possess both insight and vision. Not a few such problems the missionary will find already solved for him in the policy and experience of the Church in other and older mission fields, or in the normal laws of Church order in previous ages of Christian history. Such questions as to the conditions of admission of catechumens to baptism, or those dealing with the regulation of Christian marriage, have already been answered by an almost unanimous concensus of opinion among missionaries in other fields of missionary work. Such results of previous experience and agreed practice among various races will be a guide to the African missionary which will help him through many of his difficulties. But there are questions peculiar to this field of Central Africa to which no general ruling or catholic concensus of opinion can be adduced in answer. To such questions the missionary must find an answer which will meet his own situation and yet incur no sacrifice of Christian truth or morality. In no case is it lawful to lower the Christian standard in either of these matters, or to adopt any practice or policy which would involve sacrifice of anything vital to these matters for the sake of getting over a difficulty or making the way easier into the communion of the Christian Church. That, alas, is a temptation to which many a missionary in Africa, and elsewhere, has been often pressed to yield.

Chief among these problems is the attitude of the Evangel towards primitive native heathen practices and customs which appear to be part of their racial or tribal life, and are at the same time closely bound up with their religious faith. What is the nature of such customs? What religious idea or belief lies at their foundation, and how far are they consistent or inconsistent with the conditions and practice of Christian life and morality? These are questions that the missionary to primitive peoples is always called upon to answer. Many missionaries in different ages of missionary enterprise have looked upon such primitive customs and practice of heathen religions as of the Evil One, and called on their converts to abjure them all and sundry without distinction. Any toleration of them by the young Church was considered to be leaving a way open to the young convert of being tempted back to his old ways of heathen faith and practice. The missionary, therefore, not only preached abandonment of all such practices, but ordered the destruction of all shrines, images, and places of worship as the only safe attitude to assume and practice to follow. In this fear, therefore, the early Celtic missionaries went so far as to hew down with their axes the sacred trees or other objects round which the worship of the heathen people centred. In this they were probably right. On the other hand, we find Pope Gregory, wise and tolerant as he always was, when he sent St. Augustine to the re-conversion of England, gave him other counsel in which, though he advised the destruction of idols, advised also the preservation of their temples, "that they might be cleansed and consecrated as churches for Christian worship." In like manner also he advised the conversion of heathen feasts into festivals of the Christian Church. "For without doubt," he added, referring to the weakness of the newly made Christians, "it is impossible to cut off all things all at once from their rough minds, because, also, he who endeavours to ascend to the highest plain is elevated by steps and paces and not by leaps." Wise words that are applicable to the Evangel to-day in Central Africa as to the mission of the Apostolic Bishop in England fifteen hundred years ago.

Of course, in the early days of missionary operations among an unevangelised people, the pioneer missionary is handicapped by a lack of full knowledge of the meaning and true character of the rites, customs, and religious practice of the people. All heathen customs cannot be classed among these which the missionary is called on to condemn. Very many are part of the racial, tribal, or national life of the people, and the wise missionary will do well to endeavour to conserve as many of these as are not antagonistic to the Christian life and faith. Thus he will preserve such features of their character as may make valuable contributions to the life and history of the human race, and at the same time build up their

Christian life on a foundation that will make it the natural expression of their tribal or racial character.

Lack of this knowledge may operate in two ways. The missionary may find himself condemning practices or customs that are perfectly innocent and in no way inconsistent with the profession of the Christian faith and the practice of the Christian life. On the other hand, for the same reason, he may find himself at first tolerating practices that are vital products of their heathen life and entirely antagonistic to the Christian faith. Later and fuller knowledge, however, will enable him to differentiate between what is of the religious faith of the people and what is of tribal or racial habit and custom. In the latter case the wise missionary will not interfere.

The wearing of an amulet or tiny piece of rootlet round wrist or ankle of a baby, tied there by its anxious and careful mother, may seem only a trivial thing, and such as the mother from ignorance or in half excuse for what she fears the missionary will condemn, will describe simply as " Nothing," or " Only play." Yet on fuller knowledge the missionary will find that the " play " is really the expression of the woman's faith in the power of the charm which comes from its possession by a spirit that will counteract the influence of any spirit working or wishing ill to the infant. The mother may doubtless be ignorant of the real nature of the charm and the source of its supposed power — as ignorant as the modern motorist is of the meaning of the mascot he attaches to the radiator of his car. Yet to the mother of Central Africa the medicine twig means much, as much as the Juju of West Africa means to its devotee—it is the symbol of a great faith.

Problems that arise out of race or national custom or practice are among those that most frequently face the missionary and prove the most difficult of solution. Our knowledge of native habits and customs has greatly increased during recent years as our anthropological and ethnological studies have covered a wider field of research. Moreover, also, the African peoples, like those in almost every quarter of the globe, are beginning to realise their individuality as peoples, and to see that many of their tribal or racial customs are part of a heritage that has come down to them from their fathers and so are bound up with their life as a tribe or race. Therefore, they say, they are worthy of preservation.

In this connection, the complaint is frequently brought against the missionary of the Gospel of denationalising or deracialising the native peoples under their influence and seeking to Europeanise them into the customs, life, and habits of their teachers. Such critics compare this policy with that of the Moslem teacher of Islam. The latter interferes but little with the native practice of his converts and only prescribes certain rites and practices of the new faith. Thus the Moslem convert is not called upon to sacrifice any of the customs of his old heathen life—but simply to add to these the teachings and practices that are commanded him by his Moslem teachers. This is said, and I think with truth, to account for the spread of Islam in North and East Africa. The Christian missionary, on the other hand, calls on his convert to abandon not a few tribal practices that are inconsistent with Christian morality, and thus lays himself open to the charge of denationalising or deracialising the African.

Recently General Smuts, the South African Statesman, in his Oxford lectures on Africa, joined in this criticism of the work of Christian Missions, and to this criticism of the work of the Missions he added a criticism of the policy of Government in setting aside native modes of administration and tribal practice, which he holds to be more suitable to the African in his present stage of development than the European institutions that are replacing them. I quote his words as voicing a criticism often made by very many who, however, have no reason to give for their critisisms save repeating the parrot cry heard all over South Africa, that " missions spoil the natives." " Already," said General Smuts, " the African system was disintegrating everywhere over the whole continent. Many factors had contributed to produce this. Missionaries shared the blame with administrators : the fight against the native religious ideals had been no less destructive than the deposition of native chiefs and the institution of European organs of Government. The earlier efforts of missionary enterprise were made without any reference to a knowledge of native psychology or the light which anthropology had thrown on the past in human culture. For the Native, religion, law, natural science, social customs and institutions, all formed one blended whole which enshrined their views of the world and of the forces governing it. Attack this complex system at any point and the whole institution is endangered. The institution of the Christian religion means not only the breakdown of the beliefs in primitive spirits, in magic, in witchcraft, and the abandonment of polygamy ; it means the breakdown of the entire integral native 'weltschaunung,' or outlook on life and the world. But for the missionary, good, bad, and indifferent were met with the same ban, so long as it was not in the Bible or in the advanced practice of modern Europe. The whole tendency of the Christian Mission has been to hasten the disintegration of the native system, both in its good and in its bad aspects."

So said General Smuts. But surely if the native system were bound up, as the General says, with "magic and witchcraft and polygamy," there is only one attitude that the Christian Missionary could assume towards it. For these things he mentions are impossible under any form of Christian government, and surely also impossible in any religious system professing the Christian faith and morality.

This matter of the desire to conserve as much as possible of what is racial, or tribal or national in the old faith of the people has its dangers, and the missionary must be on the watch lest his attitude on these subjects lead his converts to belittle the difference between the old faith and the new. In not a few circles there is a tendency towards this, and unguarded statements on this subject, lauding the suitability of primitive customs to a primitive people, have had their repercussions in the foreign field. These statements have appeared in some of the home newspapers, and so rapid has been the advance in the knowledge of the English language in many parts of Central Africa that subjects discussed in the home press quickly find their way into native circles where such matters are taken up by the more advanced leaders of native opinion. Not a little of the recent trouble in Kenya, where the native church was faced with a recrudesence among its members of heathen practices which touched the roots of morality not to speak of Christian purity, in thought and feeling, arose largely from this cause. In such questions that concern any matter arising out of native habit and custom, Government is very slow to take action—even where questions of morality are involved.[1]

[1] (1) With regard to the matter that roused such interest in Christian and native circles in Kenya, I quote from a letter written to me by one of the leading missionaries: "In this instance, the Government, while by no means taking the side of reactionaries yet are unwilling to do more at this time than pass legislation to protect any young women not desirous of passing through the rites, and also parents who do not wish their daughters to be subjected to the rites. The practice they believe must die out as civilisation and education proceed,

In judging of such matters and the questions raised by them the missionary will be greatly aided by the views of the more advanced among his senior native Christians and church leaders. They know native life with all its rites and practices from the inside, and with their new outlook which Christianity has given them, they are able to appraise the real meaning of many of the customs which, in their heathen days, they followed and practised. I have ever found in such matters the views of these elders of great value in enabling one to estimate the consistency or inconsistency with Christianity of not a few of these practices that have their origin in racial, tribal, or national feeling. It is this clearer insight into the real character

but in the present crisis they have forbidden in the schools any teaching being given against the rite. Thus enlightenment taught through education is somewhat curiously forbidden by Government."

(2) In Nyasaland also recently a certain form of old heathen dance indulged in specially during the initiation ceremony of the young folks with which many objectionable practices are associated, not a few of them leading to disloyalty against all rule, both of chiefs and headmen, has recently been resuscitated and enthusiastically welcomed by the worst section of the community. The elders of the Church have protested against these dances, and a deputation of them approached the Government, but in spite of this, the Government failed to recognise these as in any way dangerous or objectionable, and refused to sanction any policy which would lead to their suppression.

of such questions that not unfrequently leads the older Christians to judge more harshly and condemn more severely than I felt justified in doing, lapses into practices that came before the native courts of the Church.

The question of how far some of these native customs can be Christianised—baptised as it were into Christian use and practice—as Pope Gregory suggested—is one that the Native Church itself will be better able to afford an answer. Certain of the rites and ceremonies with the initiation of young lads and girls into manhood and womanhood are so degrading in their nature and so destructive of all purity in thought and life that such a policy of dealing with them seems impossible. There are others again that carry with them not a little instruction which cannot fail to be helpful in their after life. Some place might be found within the course of the Church's teaching of its young hearers and catechumens for such instruction, and the rites as well as the knowledge imparted might thus be Christianised.[1]

[1] In one case in Blantyre we have adopted such a course, with results of great value to the life of wives and mothers in our Christian native community. In this case the instruction is given in private by elderly Christian women, and the rite is thus denuded of anything that makes it antagonistic to Christian morality.

The same policy might be applied to other native institutions. The Christianising of these would seem to be a more hopeful way of meeting this situation than the denationalising of them. Such a policy would do much to meet and satisfy the growing race and tribal feeling that is now of so much account in matters affecting these young peoples.

The native law of communal responsibility is one of the most widely observed of native customs, and may well be brought into the circle of Christian policy and baptised into a place as a Christian institution. Indeed, the British Government, on their entrance into the country and assuming the administration of the country, would have acted wisely had they retained this custom in native law, and given it a place in their code of Civil Administration. I have already alluded to this factor in native social life in connection with the idea of the Church. When, under the clan or tribal system, a member of the clan or tribe is held responsible for the conduct of his fellow clansmen or tribesmen there is a natural inducement for every man to use his influence in keeping the peace of the community, both for his own sake as well as for that of his fellow kinsfolk for whom he is responsible. How far this community of interest might develop into a mass movement towards the profession of Christianity on a large scale has not yet been tested. Most missionaries trained in the school of individual responsibility would look, I fancy, with suspicion on any communal movement in this direction, though the result of the preaching of the "Prophet Harris" in West Africa has shown possibilities that might lie in such movements. On a smaller scale we have seen in Blantyre not a few instances of a whole family together coming to make profession of the Christian faith—the old grandparents and parents bringing the plea, "We cannot be separated from our children in this matter."

More might be made than has been yet attempted out of this native sense of communal responsibility. The native conception of kinship, and the responsibilities of kinship widens the circle of those with whom every individual has relationships more or less close. Each member of the community has several "fathers" and "mothers," many "brothers" and "sisters," and his "children" are as numerous as the number of the younger generations within the family or clan. In reply to a friend in England who wrote to him offering to found an orphanage in his diocese, the late

Bishop Galloway of Zululand wrote, "but we have no orphans." His reply is true of all Bantuland. There are no orphans in the native sense of the word, for a child has several fathers and mothers, and an "orphanage" would only relieve these relations of responsibilities which they rarely refuse.

The changes brought about in the native community by the entrance into the country of a European Government bringing European methods of administration are further complicated by the entrance of a new class of European interests—the settlers who came as planters, traders, and other agents of commercial enterprise. In the eyes of the native the white race is one family, and consequently they were to him a community whose individuals were responsible for each others actions. For many years after the Government took over the reins of administration, the natives were with difficulty dissuaded from their belief that for all the actions of Government as well as of the other settlers, the Mission was answerable. The Mission was the pioneer of all the others who followed, and for whom in the natives' eyes the Mission was consequently responsible. It took many years of dissuasion and of experience on the natives' part before they were disabused of this idea of Mission liability for the actions of all white men in the country.

The entrance and presence of both Government and settlers have without doubt contributed both to the country and the people. The fact that Missions were the pioneers is, I believe, one of the main causes of the cordial relations that are very evident in Nyasaland between the two races, white and black. The first touch of the white race on the black was thus a touch of sympathy and goodwill, and the native judgment of the white man was favourable. This first impression the natives thus received of the goodwill of the white man towards the black has never been lost, and is one of the factors in the feeling of trust in the white man's fairness and justice which is a factor in the life of the native people to-day, and has greatly contributed to the situation in Nyasaland where there is no race problem.

And it must never be forgotten by future historians of the Central African Protectorates that the British Government, bringing with it freedom and peace, stepped in and took up the reins of power just in time. The struggle for the freedom of the Native and for his wellbeing under a Christian Government—for that was what the battles round the stockade at

Karonga meant—was one that could not have been carried on much longer. The Arab forces attacked the stockade defended by a dozen white men, traders, settlers, and missionaries, with the intention of driving out of the country all white influence and taking the reins of all native government into Arab hands. It was for both white and black together a battle for life. On the issue of the conflict depended the whole future of the Bantu race in Central Africa. It decided whether a European or Arab, Christian or Moslem, was to rule, and whether freedom or slavery was to be the future lot of these Bantu peoples.

Just in time the British Government stepped in—just in the nick of time, for the Christian side in the struggle had practically reached the limit of its resources. Their forces were well-nigh exhausted, while the Arab leaders were every day strengthening their power among the surrounding native chiefs. The situation in a few more months would have been impossible, and the forces of Christianity and civilisation would have been compelled to withdraw. The gate that Livingstone opened, and which he asked the Cambridge students not to allow to be shut again, would have been closed in our face and on a slave-driven people with none to befriend them. For the action taken by the British Government at that time, as well as for the *Pax Britannica* that followed, the cause of missionary enterprise in Central Africa cannot voice a too grateful meed of praise.

While bringing untold advantages and benefits to the country and the people, the entrance of British rule administering rule among the Natives was not without its difficulties to the missionary. Britain has endeavoured to administer her African territories for the benefit, in the first instance, of the Natives of the country. By a fiction she calls the country a Protectorate and the people not British subjects but still under the rule of their own native kings and chiefs. Yet the governing power is the Governor representing the British crown and his staff of assistants in the task. The law administered is supposed to be native law where such is not inconsistent with justice and morality. Common sense, however, in the interests of equity and fairness enters largely into the administration of the country, and the British sense of fair-play between the two races has managed to hold even the balance between white and black.

The situation, where so much is left to the good sense and discretion of the local Government official, has its difficulties for the missionary of the Church and Gospel. An instance of such difficulties arose out of the attempt on the part of the Government to deal with the question of the recognition of the Christian law of marriage among the native Christians. In native law polygamy is recognised with its rights and claims. So, too, divorce is recognised on grounds that neither British nor Christian law would admit. Succession to property in native law follows a course that British law would not allow. The Christian convert changed his whole outlook on such matters, and the Church ruled its instruction and discipline on its own Christian laws. Consequently, when such matters came up for judgment or adjustment in the native magistrates' court, native law and Christian law often found themselves in conflict. Divorces were being granted to parties married by Christian rites for grounds oftentimes wholly trivial. Much depended on the attitude of the presiding magistrate, whose sympathies might or might not be with the cause of Christian Missions. An effort was made by both missions and Government to get the Christian law of marriage—one man to one woman united for life—recognised in the native courts, and an ordinance with a view to this was passed by the local legislatives. But the administration of the new law was so lax that the law of the country, as a whole, was falling into disrepute in the eyes of the Natives and the ordinance was withdrawn. It was finally agreed that, in all civil matters connected with Christian marriage, the native courts should rule and administer justice according to native law, while the Church was left to deal with such matters as they affected the Church standing of its members according to the rule and law of the respective Churches. This adjustment has been found to work satisfactorily. But there is no doubt that as Christian institutions grow and develop on civilised lines, the present law of marriage between Christian and Christian will call for readjustment.

The missionary problem in Central Africa is further complicated by the presence of the growing number of settlers, of European and Indian nationality, who have made their homes in the country. With the latter of these two classes, the missionary has not much to do save by kindness, help, and sympathy in sickness to commend both to Hindoo and Moslem the religion he professes.[1]

[1] The Native Mission Hospitals have done much for the Indian population of both Blantyre and Zomba. The Indians

But the presence of Europeans and of European Christian congregations adds another to the problems which face the missionary in Africa.

The ideal in the life of the Church in such circumstances would be that of one Church—white and black working together for the Kingdom of God and worshipping together side by side in the Lord's House on the Lord's Day —an ideal, however, which nowhere in Central or South Africa has yet been attained. In the early days of Blantyre, when the number of Church members—both European and Native, was small, and when the sympathies of the few Scottish settlers were entirely with the missionaries in their attitude towards native Christianity, an attempt was made to secure this ideal in the Church there. At the European service, such of our native Christians as understood English attended and took part in the English service. Together they partook of the Holy Communion at the one Holy Table. It was an ideal spectacle, and as one looked at it

have built for themselves wards in both hospitals, where they come for treatment by the Mission doctors and nurses. The generosity of the Indian community in this respect shows their appreciation of what the work of the Christian missionary has done for them. Said one Hindoo merchant, alluding to the Blantyre Mission Hospital, "This is gold."

one hoped that the problem of the one Church was being solved, in Blantyre at least, and the reproach of a divided Christianity taken away.

But as the number of European settlers increased, the atmosphere in both Church and social life gradually changed. The sympathies of the outside community towards both Natives and missions gradually cooled, and the breach between colour and colour grew until it became apparent that common worship on the Lord's Day was impossible. Now in Blantyre, as elsewhere in Africa, the two races have each their own service of worship—and each congregation has its own session for the management of its own congregation's affairs. In Presbytery, however, and also in Synod, both races meet and take part, and there at least the Church is one; but alas, only there.

The breach between the two races in the Church seems universal in Africa. There is every appearance, too, of its being permanent—at least to last for a long time. Much as one laments it as a failure to reach the ideal in our Lord's mind when He prayed that all His disciples "which should afterwards believe on him might be one," yet one cannot help feeling that for the present at least it is better so. The African Native Church will be free to move forward on its own path and to work out its own ideals in life and government and on worship. In this way, I believe, she will have the way open for her to make some fresh contribution to the life of the Church as a whole that will be to its enrichment. What that contribution will be, what form it will take, "I cannot tell; God knoweth."

This at least will be seen before this century is over—and Africa will be the measure of it. This contact of black and white in the Church in Central Africa will prove to the world and to the Church itself what is the strength and real character of both the Christianity and civilisation of these times. Africa was the last of the unknown inhabited regions of the world to be opened up to the knowledge and influence that have been working so long among the civilised races of other regions. The peoples of India and China, the Arab and the European were all living, working, developing themselves and the resources of their own countries—as well as the power of their own intellectual vision—all for hundreds of years—while the African peoples sat still unknowing and unknown—hidden behind their unbroken coast line, and river marshes—making no advance. Africa was a closed land—save to the slave trader and the slave raider. Not till the slave trade has been banished from the commerce of the world's great Powers, not till they could touch Africa with clean hands, did God suffer Livingstone to go in and throw open the door into her heart. Now the Christianity and civilised influences and Powers of the world hold the reins of rule in Africa. What will they do with her? What will they make of her? Africa and what is made of Africa will be a vital test of the worth of our twentieth-century religion and civilisation. Africa throws open to them a great opportunity. How will they use it?

Remembering, then, all the past history of the African race and of all it has suffered and come through at the hands of the older, abler, and more powerful races in the human family, one has many a time asked oneself what has Africa got to bring with her into the treasury of the Church of God. I can see the great democratic races of Europe and Africa bringing their ideals of the value and responsibilities of the individual soul; I can see the Christians of India coming in with their gift of contemplation and adoration of the Divine Nature; I can see the peoples of Western Asia and North Africa restored to the Christian fold from which they were driven by the forces of Islam, coming back and bringing with them a renewed faith in the unity of the Godhead in the Trinity revealed by Jesus Christ; I can see the Christian Church of China bringing with it a reverent remembrance of the departed and of the unity in Christ of the living and the dead, and I can see the African bringing into the fold his gift of patience and that brave unmurmuring endurance of injustice and wrong which have enabled him to hold up his head amid all the horrors and cruelties of slavery and the slave traffic. I think of that. And when I remember that patience and uncomplaining endurance of wrong were seen at their highest on the Cross, I can almost hear the voice of my Lord standing by the Treasury of the Church of God and saying, as He notes the African approaching with his contribution to the Temple, "This man hath cast in more than they all."

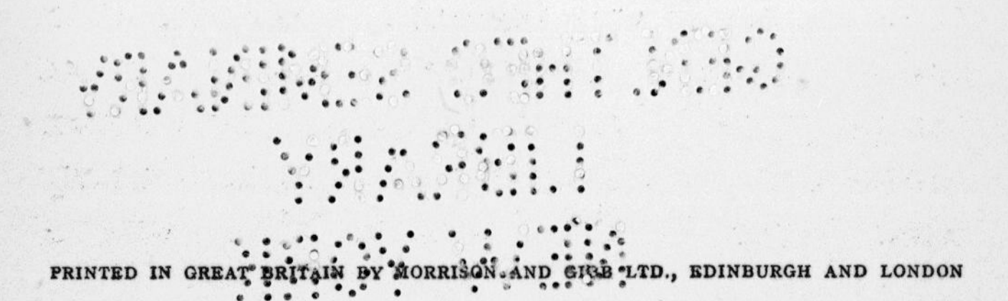

PRINTED IN GREAT BRITAIN BY MORRISON AND GIBB LTD., EDINBURGH AND LONDON